VOICES: PSYCHOANALYSIS

from the Channel 4 Television series

PSYCHOANALYSIS

Michael Ignatieff
George Steiner
Bruno Bettelheim
Steven Marcus
Hanna Segal
Arnon Bentovim
Adolf Grünbaum
André Green
Robert Young

Elizabeth Spillius
Mervyn Glasser
Jonathan Pedder
Janine Chasseguet-Smirgel
Jean Baker Miller
Juliet Mitchell
Philip Rieff
Sherry Turkle
Geoffrey Hartman

EDITED BY Bill Bourne, Udi Eichler and David Herman

SPOKESMAN
Nottingham: Atlantic Highlands
in association with
THE HOBO PRESS

First published in 1987 by:
Spokesman
Bertrand Russell House
Gamble Street
Nottingham, England
Tel. 0602 708318

and 171 First Avenue, Atlantic Highlands,
New Jersey 07716, USA
for The Hobo Press

Copyright © Brook Productions (1986) Ltd, 1987

This book is copyright under the Berne Convention. All rights are reserved. Apart from any fair dealing for the purpose of private study, research, criticism or review, as permitted under the Copyright Act, 1956, no part of this publication may be reproduced, stored in a retrieval system, or transmitted, in any form or by any means, electronic, electrical, chemical, mechanical, photocopying, recording or otherwise, without the prior permission of the copyright owner. Enquiries should be addressed to the publishers.

ISBN 0 85124 491 2
ISBN 0 86124 492 0

Printed by the Russell Press Ltd, Nottingham
(Tel. 0602 784505)

Contents

Introduction		7
1.	Freud: For or Against? *Bruno Bettelheim, George Steiner*	11
2.	Psychoanalysis: The Impossible Profession? *Mervyn Glasser, Jonathan Pedder, Elizabeth Spillius*	26
3.	Psychoanalysis: Truth or Science? *André Green, Adolf Grünbaum, Robert Young*	42
4.	Psychoanalysis: What do Women Want? *Janine Chasseguet-Smirgel, Jean Baker Miller, Juliet Mitchell*	58
5.	Psychoanalysis: Nothing Sacred? *Geoffrey Hartmann, Philip Rieff, Sherry Turkle*	73
6.	Psychoanalysis After Freud *Arnon Bentovim, Steven Marcus, Hanna Segal*	88

Introduction

Voices is a television oddity. Apparently set in a late-night Oriental carpet warehouse, it attempts to present the most exciting debates going on in the world of ideas. The debates may be topical (The New Cold War, The Future of Work) or timeless (The Mind/Brain Argument). The important thing is that they matter and deserve to reach the large audience that only television can provide.

This means going into often new and foreign terrain. New because our world is rapidly changing. Issues like Artificial Intelligence and The Post-Industrial Society are now upon us, transforming the world we live in. Developments in computer technology pose real and disturbing questions about the mind and what it means to be human. This doesn't mean taking some 'Gee Wiz' attitude to the new, but thinking through the changes and finding the voices who can make sense of this newly emerging landscape.

The humanities too have undergone tremendous upheavals in the last 20 years: new ideas, new uncertainties and even new subjects. The language of literary critics and historians is sometimes barely recognisable and has moved away from our own common sense and everyday assumptions about writing or the past. There has been a revolution in the world of criticism, undermining our older assumptions about knowledge and the self. Increasingly it is here in the world of ideas rather than in the arts, that we sense The Shock of The New.

Much of this shock is muffled by parochialism, distancing ourselves from new work by seeing it as faddish and foreign. Because so many of the great creative thinkers come from across the Atlantic or the Channel they lack any regular access to our review-pages or TV screens, and we tend to lose touch with the most important debates going on elsewhere. The important voices from abroad go unheard as if what they have to say doesn't matter. The results can be comical. When the British press finally caught up with Structuralist ideas during the row in the Cambridge English Department a few years ago, it was easy to forget that the theories at the centre of the controversy had been commonplace in Paris for 20 years. Despite the talk about 'The Global Village' intellectuals like

Chomsky or Levi-Strauss remain strangers to our screens and their ideas remain at the margin of our culture. Even more extraordinary is how rare it is on British television to find discussion of the work of British intellectuals like Edward Thompson, John Berger and Raymond Williams. There is no obvious forum for the discussion of their ideas, at a time when British intellectual culture is in fact very rich.

This is part of a growing problem of communication. Our culture has created a huge gulf between its thinkers and the rest. We take this for granted in the more arcane reaches of science and mathematics, but the same is happening in literary criticism and history and the growing areas where science touches our lives. Both academics and media have been notoriously bad at communicating the main intellectual developments of our time to the rest of us, so that like Miss Havisham we continue to live in the past, surrounded by out-of-date theories and cobwebbed assumptions.

This in turn is partly a matter of categories. Some of these debates are neither Arts, Philosophy or Science in any clear sense, but slip in between established categories. When Umberto Eco and Stuart Hall talk about a pervasive sense of crisis — is that Current Affairs? Politics? History? When Cornelius Castoriadis and Christopher Lasch talk about the breakdown of a sense of community or belonging they are not just talking about politics or sociology. These discussions are about culture in the largest sense, issues which speak to the heart of our experience, but which have no obvious home in the universities or the media.

Voices, then, tries to be alert to these problems, to this need for a forum where these kinds of issues can be discussed, and to follow an agenda which is being set by writers and intellectuals here and abroad. This agenda is often new and foreign, and may have no clear signposts. And even where there are signposts (Post-Structuralism, Post-Modernism) the question is what do they mean and why do they matter? That is perhaps a fancy way of saying: Who are the most interesting voices of our age and what do they have to say to us?

Voices has been a regular annual feature of Channel 4 since November 1982. The programme is made by Brook Productions and produced by Udi Eichler and David Herman.

One of the most interesting voices of our time has been that of Sigmund Freud. But nearly one hundred years after Freud invented psychoanalysis there is still fierce controversy about the importance of his ideas. For some, like Bruno Bettelheim, he was a brilliant thinker who opened up a new world of dreams and desires that has changed the way we think about ourselves. But for critics like George Steiner, Freud's originality has been exaggerated, and his emphasis on sexuality reductive. In some way he has actually diminished a Western tradition of introspection.

But regardless of Freud's originality, are his ideas true? Philosophers of science like Adolf Grünbaum are not so sure. Psychoanalysis is a long way from the serious world of hard science and according to Grünbaum cannot be proven or even tested. But for French psychoanalyst André Green and historian of science Robert Young, psychoanalytic understanding shouldn't be reduced like that. It offers, they say, a kind of truth that can make sense of our feelings and experiences in a way more scientific ways of thinking simply do not.

Equally heated is the debate about psychoanalysis and women. According to feminist critics like Jean Baker Miller, Freud's ideas about incest and penis envy are only the tip of a patriarchal iceberg. Women analysts Juliet Mitchell and Janine Chasseguet-Smirgel reply that psychoanalysis is interesting for women precisely because it breaks away from restricting assumptions about gender and sexuality.

Starting with Freud these discussions move into the present to look at how psychoanalysis has changed since Freud's death in 1939, both as a clinical practice ('The Impossible Profession') and as a body of theories different from other kinds of therapy ('Psychoanalysis After Freud'). And they look at Freud's legacy in a larger sense, bringing together cultural theorists like Philip Rieff, Geoffrey Hartman and Sherry Turkle to look at the impact analysis has had on our culture and values. What emerges is a debate about psychoanalysis as it is today, inside and outside the consulting room.

CHAPTER 1

Freud: For or Against
Michael Ignatieff
with Bruno Bettelheim and George Steiner

Ignatieff: Good evening, and welcome to a new series of *Voices*.

Forty-five years after Sigmund Freud's death, intense controversy surrounds his achievement and his influence on our culture. For some, he's a fanciful, even absurd, Viennese pseudo-scientist whose therapy, psychoanalysis, is little more than a clever word game for the intellectual middle classes. But for others, Freud is the most fertile and imaginative force in our culture, whose concepts, from the unconscious to the Oedipus complex, have entered the very language we use to understand ourselves and has opened up a new world of dreams, fantasy and desire which allow us for the first time to get to grips with mental illness. For the next six weeks on *Voices* we'll be trying to make sense of Freud's legacy.

We begin this week with an encounter between one of the greatest living heirs of the Viennese psychoanalytic tradition, Bruno Bettelheim, and George Steiner, a critic of psychoanalysis. Bruno Bettelheim, who first read Freud in the Vienna Woods in the 1920s, is the leading figure of the Central European migration which brought psychoanalysis to the United States. The founder of the Orthogenic School in Chicago, he's well-known for his pioneering work with disturbed children and his prolific writing on a wealth of subjects from autistic children and fairy tales to the horror of the concentration camps. Most recently he has written *Freud and Man's Soul*, a passionate defence of Freud's achievements. George Steiner has written widely on European literature, and especially on the disturbing relationship through our century between culture and barbarism. He's written scathingly of 'Freud's over-valuation of the sexual,' his 'archaic alphabet of dreams,' and perhaps in jest, has relegated him to the museum of a vanished Viennese culture.

George Steiner, I thought we should begin with the unconscious. Freud may not have discovered the unconscious, but it surely is true that his attempt to map its inner regions is both his greatest achievement and his greatest influence on our culture.

Steiner: I wouldn't for a moment disagree. The influence is enormous, all-pervasive. My own trouble is this: the impoverishment. That we have been left profoundly, radically diminished. When I think of what Coleridge meant by the limitless *terra incognita* of the self and what Aquinas, to me quite seriously a much deeper psychologist of the unconscious than Freud ever was, what Plato meant by the wealth, the dynamic wealth and multiplicity of the unconscious, and when I think of the Freudian claim for the libido, for eros, not only as important — of course it is, enormously important — but as seminal, central and finally deterministic, all determining, I cannot but have an impression that we are much the poorer, the more reduced, the more simplified for this revolution.

Ignatieff: Are you saying that he's over-sexualised the unconscious?

Steiner: Oh fantastically. Fantastically. I think the role of sexuality in numerous human beings — human beings have a very rich, complicated and creative life — is far smaller than he postulated. But I would like to give one precise example, as it were. There's a wonderful moment where Aquinas says 'how do we create something?' A great question. A poem, a painting, a piece of music. And he says one thing is certain, of course it comes from an unconscious, there's no doubt of that. From the dark area below our rational perception. But he says 'always remember, no music can come of the unmusical.' Now, what he meant by that was complicated of course and hard for us to get right, but that the forms of what he took to be the soul, the forms of the soul, of intellection, were themselves as rich, as complex and as various as what they produce.

The notion that such achievements, ideas, ideologies even, are sublimations — Freud's famous analysis — sublimations, transfers from the erotic, from a libidinal series of impulses, seems to me not only not to explain anything — Freud has never in fact explained: the famous essay on the 'Poet as Daydreamer' is, forgive me, almost childish in its contempt for literary creation, artistic creation — not only has he not explained, that wouldn't be an accusation, but got us on a very wrong track, possibly stopped us from learning more about the transit from the darkness into the light of achieved form.

Ignatieff: Now you, Bruno Bettelheim, have actually admitted in print that Freud's understanding of the artistic was often weak and diminished. But what about this specific charge that the theory of the unconscious is over-sexualised, it emphasised the libido to the exclusion of all the other forces in the unconscious?

Bettelheim: Well, everybody has to be understood both as his permanent contribution and his time-bound contribution. And if we want to understand Freud we have to understand that much of what he has worked and written and striven for was a reaction against the Victorian age and the denial of the importance of sex. And if you do battle against a denial, it's entirely possible that you over-state your case. That is part of the dynamic of a battle.

And now, what my friend George Steiner said about art, well Freud was very modest about the achievement of psychoanalysis in the field of art. He repeatedly said that it's a great mystery, at least to him, and he said that while psychoanalysis explains very adequately why somebody wants to paint and can explain that not only adequately but sufficiently, it has absolutely no answer why somebody is a Sunday painter or just put drops of paint on paper, and why somebody creates great art. And he was the first to say that as far as the riddle of creativity or creation is concerned, psychoanalysis has no answer. So his claim about sublimation is a very modest one.

Ignatieff: Ah. But I want to pursue this business about the libido. Because couldn't it be said to you, George Steiner, that the Freudian claim was modest about the theory of sublimation, but what in fact Freud was saying is, there may be a lot in the unconscious, but only repressed sexual wishes can make us *ill*? And therefore the focus on sexuality is a focus on what can actually make us wretchedly unhappy, productive of hysterical symptoms. And therefore the focus on the sexual is justified.

Steiner: I would want to be corrected here. That is not how I read him. Let's take one step back. With profound and often stoic generosity Freud several times said that Nietzsche was the greatest psychologist that had ever lived or written and that he was in some ways a footnote to Nietzsche. Let's say that to his honour, the great generosity of that remark. The will to power, Nietzche's inner driving — the Platonic, that breathtaking, intoxicating Platonic assertion that what makes us not animals but human beings is the drive to question meaning, existence — we alone ask what we do in this universe. So the notion that these various great thrusts towards being, towards self-questioning, should be infirmities, should be parts of illness, instead of, to me, the greatest strengths, the greatest sanity, whatever anguish, whatever torment it brings — and you've just put your whole finger on it — I cannot accept the notion that we have a *pathological* source here, when in fact we have the dynamics of what makes us men and women. And the notion that this is finally and deterministically sexual seems to me utterly utterly reductive and precisely parallel to Karl Marx's assertion that what it is finally all about is an economic drive. In both cases we have to do with a fundamental notion of economy, of extreme sparcity. The dynamite is one stick of dynamite, it explodes into everything. I fully accept Professor Bettelheim's point about the modesty on art, but psychoanalysis says that even ideologies, complex abstract political beliefs, religious positions, metaphysics, are products of sublimated libidinal drives. And that's insulting, I think.

Ignatieff: But I don't want to let you off the hook on this one because look at those hysterical patients of the 1880s and 90s. I mean, surely there is a discovery there of a deep sexual unhappiness? I mean, it seems to me you're simply denying the possibility that those kind of neurotic denials that those late Victorian Viennese suffered simply didn't exist or ought to be retranslated as a denied Nietzcheian will to power or something.

Steiner: No, of course not, Michael.

Ignatieff: What exactly is the claim?

Steiner: But if that was what it was about, which is a form of dentistry, we wouldn't be gathered on this programme talking about a man — what did W.H. Auden say in his wonderful poem on his death? 'No longer man, he has become the climate of our lives' opinion.' Now we wouldn't be here if that wasn't true. So I can't let you off the hook. It isn't good enough telling me he was very, very helpful to middle class, essentially Jewish, well-off hysterical ladies in a brief period of history. And footnote: we've never seen patients like Freud's again, by the way, curious footnote. Very historically limited group. No, he was a man who changed our whole civilisation, and it's not just a dental treatment.

Bettelheim: Exactly. He changed our civilisation, as you said, and I don't think we really can any longer think about man and his affliction and his achievement without use of some of the Freudian concepts and some of the Freudian approach.

Ignatieff: But specifically the thought that denies. We have many things in the unconscious that we deny, that we repress, that we forget, but the only things that can make us *ill*, that can produce neurosis, are sexual. Isn't that the core of the Freudian claim?

Bettelheim: No, not really. Because, for example, this is a very broad definition of sexual. As you know, I've worked with very disturbed children, and in many cases their biggest problem is their relationship to their parents. Or their parents' relationship to them.

Ignatieff: But that's not a sexual matter, that's a matter of their relation to authority, for example.

Bettelheim: Well, or hatred or lack of love or rejection or whatever you call it. And while Freud mostly concentrated on the libido, on the sexual aspects, because I think that was a reaction to the Victorian age, and a very necessary reaction to the Victorian denial of the importance of the sexual. Or the dishonesty in talking about the sexual.

Ignatieff: Yes.

Bettelheim: But on the other hand, what we now know about sibling rivalry, what we know about, say — call it Oedipal or whatever you want — the relationship between children and their parents and parents' ambivalent relationship to their children and how destructive that is, we wouldn't know without Freud.

Steiner: I would like first of all just — and I'm not challenging, I'm thinking out loud — how much more do we know about sibling rivalry than was known to the authors of the Old Testament and of Esau and Jacob? How much more do we know about children and parents than was known to Shakespeare when he wrote King Lear? So the actual use of the word 'know' troubles me. What there is in Freud's great achievement that is new knowledge, I think we may be too close to the event. Because the insights have been expounded by great imaginers, writers and philosophers, though not systematically, for a very long time. It's not like saying that in Einstein the first answer to the perihelian of Mercury against Newton, that is possibly new knowledge. Though I know philosophers would make that statement very carefully only. The word 'know' is difficult.

Let me come to the central example, on which Bruno Bettelheim has himself written very movingly and very deeply, the Oedipus business. That is much more than a suggestion, it permeates civilisation, I would say, today. Even those who have never read Freud are surrounded by its presence. I remain utterly and helplessly unconvinced as to its universality in other cultures. Freud never answered Malinowski's challenge and the other challenges of anthropology on its Western singularity. Secondly, and at the risk of total derision from everyone here in our audience, I have desperately tried, desperately, to find in myself hatred of my father, who was my very best friend I've ever had in my life, and sexual desire for my mother, whom I lost only a few years ago. I've desperately tried to find it. I really wanted to be *à la page*, in the calendar of modern civilisation. I've utterly failed. That is trivial.

Now we come to the worrying point. If you say this, not to someone of the deep humanity of Bettelheim, but say it to the average psychoanalytically convinced person, he says that's the very proof of your suppression. In other words, Catch 22. We cannot argue honestly against that dogma.

Bettelheim: Yes, but you can't accuse me of an argument that I haven't made. I think it's very convenient to do so, but I cannot accept the challenge. Now, let me try to answer a few things. True, Freud has not talked about other cultures. And as a matter of fact, in the one important work, *Totem and Taboo* in which he talked about it, he made many mistakes, many errors. Why? Because he relied on the anthropology of his days. He didn't rely on the anthropology of today. And I think it's pointless to argue that. On the other hand, he has given us insight into how the taboo works and why it works, which were entirely novel at the time, and have now entered anthropology as a basic principle.

Now, about the Oedipus complex: of course the Oedipus complex or the Oedipal relation have to do with the dominant role of the father. Otherwise it doesn't make any sense. Therefore it all played out who is the dominant figure in the life of the child. In Freud's time, the paternalistic culture of Central Europe and Western Europe, it was the father. So that's what he talked about. But if you read Freud it's quite clear that it's a dominant role, it's a great power the father held over his children, and therefore the anxiety and the ambivalent feelings that are created in anybody who is subjected to the power and the arbitrariness of a very important figure in his life. So it all depends how you read Freud. Now, Freud was the first who said that he didn't invent what he tried to teach. He just tried to understand it in a different way. He not only mentioned Nietzsche, he mentioned Dostoyevsky, that he knew all that psychoanalysis could teach. That is, that the artists always have known it. And all the great teachers of mankind, if you like. And when you speak about the Bible, if you look at the great story of sibling rivalry, the Joseph legend in the Old Testament, it is not quite clear there. It's intimated, but it's not quite yet worked out why the brothers were so jealous of Joseph. Nor does it really make it clear how destructive the father's preference for Joseph was to Joseph. That is, this kind of tragedy was not worked out. Because it's a story, it's a myth, a legend. Or, if you like, the Bible.

Ignatieff: But how do you meet George Steiner's objection? What does Freud teach us that we didn't already know in the Jacob and Esau story in relation to brothers and that we didn't know in relation to King Lear and his daughters? That is, what is novel and new, what's the achievement of Freud in relation to that tradition?

Bettelheim: I think, as an educator. I think it's a great advantage that now many parents are aware that they have ambivalent feelings about their children. That is something that in the great literature you found all the time, but the average parent, the average mother and father, did not know that and they were helpless when they encountered these feelings in themselves. They thought they are evil. But now they know this is part of an intimate relation, that it has ambivalent features. And that we owe to Freud. So that I believe is a humanisation of human relations.

Ignatieff: Yes. But let's turn the heat on you, George Steiner, for a minute. You've made some very mordant and, it seems to me, penetrating criticisms of both Freud's relation to the pre-Freudian tradition in relation to the unconscious, and some criticism in relation to the theory of the unconscious. And those are criticisms about his relation to the tradition, criticisms in relation to theory. But what do you say to the millions of people who've embarked on psychoanalysis as a therapy? That is, who can say to you 'look,

George Steiner, I don't always agree with the theory myself, but this man has changed my life. On the couch, five days a week, I have enabled myself to confront myself in ways that were never possible before.' Are these people simply deluded?

Steiner: I would like to answer on two levels. *The Delusion*, the title of a very famous study of mass delusion; more people were involved with a belief in witchcraft over centuries in Europe, the belief in exorcism, the belief in certain rituals and rites of therapy, than even perhaps are involved with psychoanalysis, which let us not forget, has not reached three-fifths of humanity: the underdeveloped world, barely China and Russia and so on. First of all, this question of a mass belief, a mass imagining — and with all due respect, absolutely nothing libellous meant — let us do some thinking after your question on the enormous spread of certain fundamentalist religious sects now who come from door to door, the Mormons, Jehovah's Witnesses, certain extreme Baptists. So first of all, the statement 'a lot of people will tell you that's what they want,' doesn't, alas, move me either way. I believe them. I say 'good luck to you,' and it would be absolutely impertinent not to.

The other thing, the other part of the statement, is of course much more complex. What *is* this thing? Has it cured anyone? There's much debate on this. Can I come back for a moment, in the light of your question, to the Oedipus complex? Someone whom both Bruno Bettelheim and I very much admire, the great Austrian novelist, thinker and philosopher, Musil. This came up at a luncheon party in Vienna — we have the exact date and so on — where Musil, like myself, said he had searched and searched in himself for sexual desire of the mother and the parricidal impulse but could not find it. And the classical answer was given, not by Dr Bettelheim, but by perhaps a much lesser figure: 'this is the best proof we have of how rich is the drive you're suppressing.' And what worries me so deeply about the psychoanalytic enterprise is the cut-off point where you lose either way. You cannot win the argument, because the fact that you argue is the best evidence. And this lands you in very primitive dogmatics of a peculiarly intolerant kind. We have needed a Voltaire very, very badly. We don't have him.

Bettelheim: Well I think the argument that you deny it proves it is a silly argument, and I don't think that anybody of any intelligence will use it but as a joke. That some people take jokes seriously is due to the limitations of their intelligence.

Ignatieff: What about the issue of therapy?

Bettelheim: About the therapy, firstly, there have been experiments made into what it does to have a person lie down one hour, the same hour every week, five times a week or six times a week and introspect, and the results are quite remarkable. Now I think—

Ignatieff: That is — just to interrupt, this is introspection without a Freudian context?

Bettleheim: Without. But the same time, and regularly.

Ignatieff: Yes.

Bettelheim: To be forced to take 50 minutes or an hour off from a busy life, lie down on the couch, without any distraction, without interruption, without any stimulation from the outside and to reflect on yourself. And it's quite remarkable what it does. When people talk about meditation, you know, sometimes it's very shallow, but for some people it is really serious thinking things through and mulling things over.

Ignatieff: So if it does you good even if you do it alone, what's the point of the analyst?

Bettelheim: As I come to that. Sigfried Bernfeld has said really the best thing about this self-analysis, as it's called. He said the only difficulty — 'self-analysis, wonderful, there's only one thing wrong with it, and that's the counter-transference.'

Ignatieff: Counter-transference to yourself?

Bettelheim: That's right. And that is very interesting, that Bernfeld said that because he re-analysed some of the dreams Freud had analysed in his *Interpretation of Dreams* —

Ignatieff: His own dreams?

Bettelheim: Freud's dreams. And could demonstrate from the material that Freud didn't carry the analysis far enough because of personal inhibitions, personal resistances, whatever you may call it. So we have here a classic from a Freudian point of view, a re-analysis of the classic examples of dream analysis, which showed that even a Freud couldn't carry self-analysis far enough. So therefore the same could be seen in the experiment. People were put on the couch, you know, and somebody recorded, and some of them were even meant to believe that an analyst is listening, although nobody was listening. And quite interesting insights into oneself come to light. Now you could say that has happened since the beginning of time. You are absolutely right. But since the beginning of time there were only rarely fairly skilled people listening and pointing out where self-love stopped one seeing what one's own productions were.

Ignatieff: Well there's a defence of therapy which links it to the whole European tradition of introspection and makes it something a little more dignified than witchcraft, delusion. What do you say to that?

Steiner: I think we've now either stumbled or by great wisdom come upon the centre of the disagreement. There's a remark by

Pascal, that if a human being can sit alone and quietly on a chair in a quiet room he can be saved. And that is not said lightly, that that is the act of grace.

Ignatieff: And most can't, Pascal goes on to say.

Steiner: Most can't, and as a teacher I have for over 30 years had only one job, I think, to help people achieve this. That is to say, to find their inner ballast, or even to read a book quietly or even to listen to some music without reading at the same time or watching the television screen. This is, I think, where the thing gets really central. Has Freud and has psychoanalysis added to the inner baggage of our insight into our limitations of our powers of concentration and privacy, or has he on the contrary, and particularly by the introduction of the paid listener — I want to emphasise this — I will immediately come to the crucial point, of the 60 minute convention —

Bettelheim: 50 minute, 50 minutes.

Steiner: 50 minutes. Forgive me, rates have gone up. Has he in fact scattered the reserves of discretion, of self-confidence and of stoic inner toughness, even, I would say, creative self-contempt, which to me mark an adult human being? Where I simply don't follow Bruno Bettelheim is that we have in this discussion taken it for granted that knowing more about ourselves is a marvellous desideratum and a great goal.

Let me put it in a deliberately over-simplified and extreme way. As a scholar and teacher, if somebody comes to me and says 'I want to give my life to 9th century Chinese bronze chamber pots, and I won't apologise and I won't negotiate,' Nietzsche said 'beyond love, beyond hate, beyond death is that which interests us,' which is, I think, absolutely cardinal, even beyond death.

Ignatieff: Even if it's 9th century Chinese pots.

Steiner: I don't care what it is. That person is in a state of grace, because he will contribute to something greater than himself, an ongoing life of the mind and of knowledge. Most of us, when we look into ourselves, there's almost nothing there, or it's shabby, trivial and second-rate. No, I mean this very seriously, not as a debating point. What is this unexamined desideratum of self-revelation? Most of us are a titanic bore.

Bettelheim: No, I can't agree to that. I have never yet found anybody whom I've found a bore. I found them boring only as long as we don't penetrate beyond the surface. I've found every human life extremely interesting, fascinating. And I learned from it and the other subject learns from it. I don't believe they're telling me lies when they say they have learned from it and gained a great deal in self-understanding. I really believe that, as Plato or Socrates said, that the unexamined life is not worth living. Now, psychoanalysis is one way to examine one's own life. And that is its tremendous merit. Now, we cannot predict what somebody will do with this examination. We all know patients who go on *ad infinitum*, which is really a self-defeating enterprise. And we know others who have changed their life, and they think for the better. And who are we to doubt that? I don't have this Olympian judgement that I know what people ought to do, what people ought to feel, what people ought to think, how they ought to spend their time. I only know that I haven't found anybody yet, in my experience, who regretted the time they spent on this self-examination.

Steiner: Now I want to be much more democratic for a moment even than you. You have written with immemorial poignancy and insight. Your book was one which when I was very young and had the privilege of knowing you scarcely out of school, simply formed me, *The Informed Heart*. And one must always quote against a person their own finding. And one of the points you make in that marvellous book is the unsuspected resources of strengths and of creative resistance in ordinary people under terrible circumstances.

I would like to draw you on this. We aren't talking just of creativity. It's precisely, I think, the terribly demanding task of coming to terms alone with oneself, with the material of darkness, of frustration, of mendacity, in oneself. If you can get through that tunnel, then there is a strength and an at-homeness in one's failures. To be grown up is to know how badly one has failed oneself and others and the people one loves. At every level.

Now this discovery, this very hard task, which was the great discipline of silence in previous centuries, the letter writing by hand, the diary writings, the attempt to be oneself in the face of that kind of pressure, it seems to me, psychoanalysis, while saying you must do it, has institutionalised a certain kind of self-avoidance. This is where I don't agree with you. It cannot be an accident that it is massively related in the United States to a culture which has been called the culture of confession, the culture of saying all.

Bettelheim: Of the therapeutic.

Steiner: There are many words for it. Is not a human being — you have spoken of it in the extreme position of the death camps — but many other situations, I've watched you work with autistic children in your clinic — is the real task not precisely the one of having to do it oneself?

Bettelheim: I'm perfectly willing to accept that each period has its own way to institutionalise cathartic methods, shall we say? Ways to get insight into oneself, to be confronted with oneself. And as George Steiner, and I appreciate that, quotes me, I said in the concentration camps one was confronted with oneself. Not everybody, but quite a few people. An extreme situation, a very severe trauma, people who have been in danger of their lives report, some, not all, that their life was changed by it. So there are many situations where people are confronted with themselves. In our time and age, the most widespread method to be confronted with oneself is psychoanalysis, that's all.

Steiner: Widespread, but may I again say—

Bettelheim: I know, within this Western culture, yeah, yeah, and not behind the iron curtain.

Steiner: No. But no, this is important. Now, this, I think, is worth thinking about for a moment. If, for example, you are in a very oral culture, which is the Soviet culture, which learns by heart, continually and massively, where poetry is spoken from person to person, from mouth to mouth — the great form of resistance is to learn by heart — what strikes one in that image, as against our mimeograph and word processor kitsch culture, what strikes one in that image is the baggage you put inside you for the journey. The journey which can take you to illness, to divorce, to the deaths of those closest to one, to the most terrible personal errors and catastrophes, or to the camp or to the prison, or to whatever.

Now, this journey, what luggage should we take with us? And what strikes me in the great inheritance of psychoanalysis, and particularly in the United States, is that the luggage is getting emptier. It is being emptied out in the psychoanalytic process and the private resources, the reserves of secrecy. There is somewhere a marvellous remark in one of the earliest fragments, not in Sophocles, another Antigone fragment, which said 'what makes a human being invulnerable: a great secret.' It's a remark which haunts me a lot. That you carry in yourself, almost as a woman carries a child, that which you have to live with. And it is the crust of the secret which the analytic method seeks to break open into the light. My own hunch is that it is secrets which make us creatively what we are. All of us, not just the great artists.

Bettelheim: Well, I don't want to argue that. For the following reason: because while you discover things about yourself in analysis, there's a reason why we analysts say that the effectiveness or the proof of the success of the analysis does not become apparent till about a year to two years — and more likely two years — after the end of analysis. That is, there is certain work that has to be done by yourself without the help of the analyst. Some insights have to be yours. Whether you say them in front of the analyst or not is not all that important. They have to be *your* discoveries. They can't be anybody else's discovery.

Therefore, the image of the psychoanalyst who knows all the answers is one of the most damaging and erroneous images. And Theodor Reik, you know, one of Freud's students, has written a book *The Surprised Psychologist — or Analyst*. That is, the most important insights of the patient are to some degree surprises to the analyst. Because anything the analyst could know does not go to the real deepest heart of the matter.

Steiner: But could I come back, at the risk of being cut off, to this central question of privacy? There's a poem by Ezra Pound, 'Hugh Selwyn Mauberly', one of those formidably prophetic poems which that bizarre but sometimes illuminate man wrote, where he said that 'there lies ahead an age of frankness as never before.' 'Frankness', he didn't mean it as a compliment. And immediately then he says 'a tawdry cheapness shall invade our days'.

Ignatieff: What precisely are the links between this and Freud?

Steiner: As Professor Bettelheim has said, the great reaction against Victorian taboos. Also verbal taboos. I've never agreed with this, that the Victorians were that taboo-ridden, but that's not what we're discussing. You've only to look at much of their literature. I believe that George Eliot — I'm really going to make a stand — there's a marvellous scene in *Middlemarch*, that most mature and grown-up of English novels, two people are back from a honeymoon, she doesn't tell us that. She wants us to understand that it's a catastrophe. They go up the stairs and she suddenly has an image that in that house the damp seemed to spread from the one human being to the other, one of the most powerful sexual images. That's all she needs to say. She honours me as a grown-up, she honours herself as a grown-up, and most important she honours the privacy of her personages. Which means she can create living, independent beings. In our culture, where analysis says do not be afraid of sexuality, hang it out, the dreadful American phrase—

Bettelheim: Freud never said 'hang it out.'

Steiner: Freud would never have said 'hang it out.' The movement has overwhelmingly said it. And we are indeed in a culture where everything can be said. I think it is a much more boring and much weaker culture than a culture of reticence. But there I've made myself as vulnerable as I can. And I cannot dissociate from this the immense genius, himself a stoic, very reticent man, Freud, who never liked an off-colour joke to be said—

Bettelheim: That's right.

Steiner: — the paradox is what has been done in his name since.

Ignatieff: What do you say?

Bettelheim: Firstly that Freud, as George Steiner correctly said, was an extremely private man. That he made it a point twice in his life to destroy all his private papers. He wanted his private papers to be destroyed after his death. When Marie Bonaparte acquired his letters to Fliess he asked her to destroy them. And so he felt very strongly that his private life was a private affair, and he felt that about anybody else.

Ignatieff: But apart from Freud the man, what do you say to the argument that psychoanalysis has encouraged a cultural movement through modern society towards a kind of excessive explicitness, an excessive revealing of the private?

Bettelheim: I think there we go to the problem of mass society. I think Mr Steiner represents a very elitist point of view. I find it very attractive. But that's a personal statement.

Ignatieff: Why elitist? I don't follow why it's elitist.

Bettelheim: Because I think it takes a certain cultural background and a certain education to be able to do all these things that Mr Steiner values so highly. I think in a mass culture you have to pay a price. The price unfortunately has for some time to be vulgarisation. I hope it's not a permanent price. I can't predict the future. I very much hope that education will spread, culture will spread to ever broader circles of the population. Most of all that more people will have the leisure, the free time to engage in cultural pursuits.

But Freud said we can talk about everything in the right way, and his insistence on the confidentiality, insistence that the analyst is never to talk about what the patient tells him. As a matter of fact he'd better forget it after a while. So he was very well aware that certain things have to remain private if we want to keep our own dignity.

a certain moment in culture. Possibly one of the finest artists of myth and instinctive — why does he ask Thomas Mann to be the one to honour him for his birthday? Because in Mann's *Joseph and His Brothers* he has found a brother creator of myth. Freud himself, a master of myth, and in that incomparable. But now, we who are not he, who do not have his ironies, who do not have his bleakness in front of what can be achieved—

Bettelheim: His self-irony also.

Steiner: — his self-ironies — may be in a position where we are, unless we're very careful, the poorer, not for *his* work, but for what we're doing with it. I would like to put it that way.

Ignatieff: But let's sharpen this up, because you've both been remarkably charitable and humane with each other, but if we strip it away, what I hear George Steiner saying is that you, Bruno Bettelheim, have pledged your life to a late 19th century cultural fashion which is now having almost entirely nefarious effects on modern culture. Now surely you can't sit here and be agreeable in the face of that?

Bettelheim: Oh I can be very agreeable, you know. After all, Freud himself said there's no point in arguing. Let the evidence, or let the findings, or let the experience of the individual decide. And I was fortunate enough on the basis of my psychoanalytic training and experience to help children to be restored to a useful life who were otherwise destined to spend their life in the back yards, as vegetables in the back yards of a mental institution. And I think that benefited them. And nobody, on a different basis than on the psychoanalytic understanding of what ails them, what was their tragedy, was able to help such children. That's on which I stake the merit or demerit of what I've been doing.

Steiner: But I would like to come to your aid in terms of sharpening. If I've understood Bruno Bettelheim entirely justly this afternoon, give or take particular cases, he does seem to feel that just about everybody who can, who freely wishes, should be psychoanalysed.

Bettelheim: No, no.

Steiner: Have I misunderstood you on that?

Bettelheim: No, I don't think everybody should be psychoanalysed. I think this is a horrible thought. As a matter of fact, even Freud never thought of that. The biggest claim he ever made was that if teachers would be analysed, and therefore would educate the future generation in a more enlightened way, this was the best he hoped for psychoanalysis to achieve. So that is a very limited goal. I think Freud would have been flabbergasted at the idea that everybody should be analysed. He was elitist and psychoanalysis is an elitist enterprise. It takes a lot of time, a lot of free time, a lot of concentration on the self, a lot of concentration on the human mind — and I hope that's something you will appreciate — a single-minded concentration on oneself and on one's own development into a richer personality. Because unless psychoanalysis achieves that, it achieves nothing.

Steiner: Well, this allows me to say, if I may, as a teacher, and there we really are on central ground, my wish is very different from yours, and the list of priorities I can think of, particularly for the secondary school system in the emancipated West at the moment, would be radically one away from psychoanalysis and towards trying on the contrary enormously to increase the resources of privacy and the sense of mystery in front of that which in us is insoluble. So there we really possibly have a respectful difference of a fundamental kind.

Bettelheim: May I say one more thing to that? I hope you both have seen photographs of Freud's study and his treatment room. They were small, private, archaeological museums. Freud — it wasn't a hobby, he really studied it very seriously — devoted much of his free time, and much more money than he could afford on the acquisition of archaeological objects, of the antique, but not only Greece and Rome, but also Egypt. Over the analytic couch hung a huge photograph of Abu Simbel, which reflects something of the importance of death and burials, and many of the artefacts on his desk and his study were from burial sites. This was a declaration that psychoanalysis is archaeology. The archaeology of the individual. So, while in a way you could say he didn't pay much attention to the particular cultural background of his patients, he emphasised the importance of history. World history and individual history. And, so to say, advertised it by the way he arranged his study and his treatment room.

Steiner: In China they now know that further hills in the western tomb region contain treasures, perhaps a hundred and a thousandfold beyond the ones already fantastically excavated and the Chinese have decided *not* to open them. A complex decision, which I find profoundly persuasive and moving. They say first of all there is enough for us to dream and think and study about for centuries. Secondly, it is enormously important and interesting that they be there, unseen by us. We are turning round an image perhaps, the archaeological image of that which when you bring it to the surface, it falls into dust, or it dies in a museum glass box. And that image might at least also remain open between us when we apply it to the resources buried in ourselves.

Ignatieff: I think, with this set of archaeological images, very touching images from China and from that study in 19 Bergasse, we should end this discussion. It'd be foolish of me to summarise it, but I'm very struck by one simple difference between George Steiner, who seems to feel that in many ways the whole Western tradition of self-interpretation, self-reflection, has been curiously and subtly diminished by the Freudian contribution at the end of the 19th century, and the Bruno Bettelheim view, which is that in many ways this is the tradition from which Freud comes and this is the tradition he left immeasurably enriched.

CHAPTER 2

Psychoanalysis: The Impossible Profession?

Michael Ignatieff with Elizabeth Spillius
Mervyn Glasser and Jonathan Pedder

Ignatieff: Good evening. Psychoanalysis has provided a hugely influential body of ideas about the self and culture. But above all it's a therapy, a way of treating human unhappiness. Tonight, we want to get a little bit closer to the therapeutic experience at the heart of psychoanalysis, to find out what actually goes on between patient and analyst in consulting rooms all over the country. To discuss what one famous analyst has called 'the impossible profession', we have three distinguished British analysts from each of the main schools of psychoanalysis: Mervyn Glasser, who's a consultant psychiatrist at the Portman clinic in London and is a leading 'B' group analyst; Jonathan Pedder, consultant psychotherapist at the Maudsley Hospital in London and a leading member of the independent school; and Elizabeth Spillius, a leading Kleinian analyst.

Ladies and gentlemen, this is a chance for me. I have three analysts, a captive audience, and I want to pretend that I am a potential patient, a potential analysand, and I want you to tell me, beginning with Jonathan Pedder, why it is that I should choose psychoanalysis as opposed to any other therapy that I might choose, to meet my distress? What is it about psychoanalysis that makes it different from other kinds of therapy?

Pedder: I think we have to go back a step and think why psychotherapy of any kind is a way of solving people's emotional discomfort and distress rather than turning to drugs or alcohol? And I think it's part of a very long historical tradition of seeking self-knowledge, fulfilling the ancient Delphic injunction 'know thyself', which has been sharpened up in a particular modern form via the insights that Freud developed through psychoanalysis. Because I think all forms of dynamic psychotherapy today, individual, group and so on, many of them lean a lot on psychoanalytic insights in the work of Freud. So then if you say why psychoanalysis rather than some other form of analytic psychotherapy, I would say because that provides the most radical and intensive opportunity of a thorough attempt at gaining that kind of self-knowledge.

Ignatieff: Why radical? What's radical about it?

Glasser: What's radical about it really is that it has a position which it sticks to very firmly, and that is that it has a profound respect for the individual. That's its radical position, that it will take no step back from that situation.

Ignatieff: I still don't see what distinguishes psychoanalysis from other forms of therapy, because other forms of therapy might say we pay the same attention to the individual, we take the same respect to the individual.

Glasser: Well, they might say so, but I think in the actual technique and the actual relationship to the patient they don't do it to that extent. An analyst is trained not only to listen to everything a patient says, but in a way to listen to what the patient doesn't say. Every detail, every movement, everything which betrays the individual idiosyncratic self of that person is what the analyst is concerned with, so that the individual realises himself.

Ignatieff: Elizabeth Spillius, help me out here. What is it about psychoanalysis that makes it different from the other therapies?

Spillius: Well, there are three things basically that I think are characteristic of analysis. One is that it's based on an understanding of the unconscious. And I think actually that it wasn't Freud's discovery, but it certainly was he who systematised the way of thinking about it and using the idea therapeutically, and of course it's now spread to a great many other psychotherapies as well. I think the second is the notion of defence. That is, that everybody has very primitive feelings and anxieties which, in adulthood, but originating in infancy, are quite difficult for them to bear, and that they have developed some kind of arrangement either to keep these unconscious or to find some way of expressing them, often quite awkward and inconvenient ways, such that they won't really have to face the raw experience of their most primitive feelings and anxieties. And the third is the notion of transference, and that's such a basic idea in analysis that I think we have to look at it a bit more.

Ignatieff: Define transference if you can, toughest question there is in psychoanalysis.

Spillius: Yes, in half a sentence! Well it began, or rather I think most people's idea of it, if they're not very well acquainted with analysis, is that it means being in love with one's analyst. And indeed, when Freud first began talking about it intensively, that was the main example that he gave. But he was very concerned at the time to point out that this wasn't a real love. In fact, that it had a defensive function. It was to keep people off the problems that really they should have been pursuing, according to him, and they were so much in love with him that they couldn't get on with the job.

Now that certainly is an aspect. And I think it crops up quite explicitly like that in many analyses. But we now think of it in much more general terms. That is that these anxieties, fears that I spoke of, dating from infancy, stay with one in some form or other, and that they repeat themselves in all one's later social relationships.

What happens, in effect, is that in normal social interaction the expectations that one has, deriving from one's early experience, are constantly being corrected by the way other people behave. Whereas in analysis it's a bit different, because the analyst doesn't behave like other people do. He is more detached. In some ways apparently more unresponsive. And therefore the transference has a chance to develop and become more explicit, more open, and both analyst and patient together can look at what the patient is feeling and examine both the way it feels now, in the present with the analyst, and its connection with early childhood experiences at the same time.

Ignatieff: Is that how you would define transference, would you like to add something to that or dissent?

Pedder: I like to see it in both general and specific terms. I think I agree with everything that was said about the way it develops in an analysis, but in case it still seems a mysterious phenomenon, I like to see it in a general context. Janet Malcolm has got a nice phrase for it, describing transference as how we all invent each other according to early blueprints. If you don't know anybody very well, you're not given many cues, you're bound to imagine certain things about them. Same as if we look at the clouds on a dark night, we may see faces in them. We imagine things all the time. So this is a general psychological phenomenon. We're always reading things into situations. And then this is intensified in psychoanalysis by the relative inactivity of the analyst, the analyst sitting behind the couch and so forth — other things we'll maybe come onto — these intensify transference, within what Pontalis, the French analyst, has called the 'private theatre of transference.' They bring it to life in a particularly vivid way.

Ignatieff: All right, if we return to my first question, what seems distinctive about psychoanalysis is this very intense, sustained, protracted relationship between analyst and patient, concentrating on the individual, as you say, working through these defences in a transference relationship. Now, a lot of what you say is very puzzling to a layman. 'An analyst doesn't behave like other people,' you said. Now what as practising therapists do you mean by that? Do you feel you have to pull back from a patient, deliberately withdraw sympathy and empathy? What is it that you're doing as a listening person — because it's a listening job you have — that makes it so different from other forms of listening?

Spillius: Well, I think there are two qualities that one has to have. One is an acute kind of listening and taking in, with great curiosity, always half-asking the question 'why is this happening now? What does it mean?' And that involves two attitudes. They seem contrasting, but they have both got to be there, I think. One is empathy. Enough of imagining oneself in the position of the patient to feel what it is that he or she might be feeling. The other is analytic. I'm not meaning psychoanalytic, I mean analytic in the general sense: look at it at the same time. So that on the one hand there is detachment and a great deal of thought. On the other hand there is empathy and a great deal of feeling. Now these two have got to be integrated. I mean, it sounds like a rather perfectionist description. But I think that's the attitude of mind, or one aspect of the attitude of mind, not by any means the only one, that an analyst needs to have when working.

Ignatieff: But how do you convey this empathy? You see, as a layman, my experience, my image of psychoanalysis is of a very cold, watchful presence behind that couch, who may understand, but whose empathy may be strictly beside the point, and in any case seems to me rarely conveyed. What I want to know is how you actually convey it to a patient who's, after all, in the midst of what is often a terrifying or a difficult experience. And how is empathy actualised or made real in a clinical situation?

Spillius: I would make a distinction, and it's perhaps not exactly a valid one, between empathy and sympathy. Because I think that in a sense to say to a patient 'oh poor you' or 'you have been a victim all your life,' may be relevant sometimes but the real thing one is aiming at is understanding. And the sense that a patient gets of an analyst being understanding in both senses, of intellectual understanding and emotional understanding, doesn't come, I think, from overt expressions of sympathy. It comes from understanding something in themselves that they've never been able to understand or especially to accept in themselves. And over time a feeling of the analyst actually helping, without making it explicit and saying, 'I'm in sympathy with you. I like you. Yes, I understand what you feel,' but actually being able to help the patient to be more insightful about himself, gives a feeling of 'this person basically is with me, wants to help me.'

Glasser: Well, I was just thinking how difficult it is to generalise, and it comes back to my point about it being concerned with the individual, that with each individual you're different. And you'll be more — to use your distinction — sympathetic with one patient than you might be with another patient. Because it's needed. I think what you can feel confident that one patient can journey, that a patient can travel with you just sort of walking along with him or her, with another patient you've got to be standing more closely with him or her. Or giving more support.

Ignatieff: But negatively, isn't it possible that there are some patients for whom no empathy is possible and therefore psychoanalysis is not advisable?

Glasser: I just can't believe that. With the most awful character, socially speaking, once you get to know them internally, you cannot but help see their humanity. When I think of myself working with a patient there's a process of going somewhere with that patient, in terms of what's absorbing them and what's worrying them or what they're talking about, and you're trying to understand it and place it in terms of your overall work concept. And it's not so much a question of like or dislike, which is different from empathy. Empathy is a question of knowing what they're feeling through feeling it yourself. I don't think like or dislike very strongly comes into it really.

Spillius: Oh, I think it often does. And I often find it very useful in understanding what's going on. For example, I had a patient once, a woman, who often was stirring me into some kind of dislike, or to put it more factually, I would have impulses of thinking 'I don't like this person.' Then I had to think why? What does this mean? What's going on here? And after a good deal of thinking and feeling things out, I came to the conclusion that what was happening was that she was getting me to experience something that she had felt in her early childhood towards someone else, a nanny in fact. So that most of the things that she was enacting and that I was feeling so negative about were actually her way of telling me about her past, but she couldn't put it into words. She couldn't describe it, it was too early for that. But she was making me feel it. And once I'd understood that, then I was less uptight about disliking her and we began to understand what was happening.

Ignatieff: One of the things that you're all saying in a certain way is that the analysis of a patient is a constant self-analysis of your reactions to the patient.

Spillius: Indeed.

Ignatieff: And you say it's such a difficult thing to do. Can you amplify on that, the sense that it's difficult? Because a layman might think all you do is sit behind a couch and listen to someone rabbit on.

Spillius: I wish.

Ignatieff: Why is it so hard?

Spillius: Well, can I introduce another technical term?

Ignatieff: Well, try.

Spillius: Counter-transference.

Ignatieff: Counter-transference?

Spillius: Right. Originally thought of as a counterpart to transference, of course, hence the name. And thought of as something pathological in the analyst for which he should go away and get more analysis and then he would stop doing it and would be neutral etc etc.

Ignatieff: Give us an example of counter-transference feelings, just in the abstract. What are you talking about?

Spillius: Oh well, say a dislike of a patient so extreme that one could hardly think in a session. That's very crude. Or a liking so extreme that you couldn't think very well is equally awkward, even more so. Now, originally and still by many people, that's the definition of counter-transference. But gradually it's come to be used more widely. That is, to be used to mean the analyst's emotional response to the patient. Now, what's hard work in analysis is that one has to use that all the time, and constantly be thinking, as I had to with the person I did —

Ignatieff: What do you mean, use it?

Spillius: Well, not just say, 'well, I don't like this person,' or 'I'm very fond of this patient,' and so on and so on, but actually think from what I know of myself why is this feeling getting stirred up in me now? And what does it mean about the patient as well as what does it mean about me? And to keep those apart and yet be able to see them both at the same time.

Ignatieff: So far we've talked of your profession as a listening profession. You have to develop very sensitive antennae to what people are saying. You also have to have a kind of constant introspective capacity to listen and feel your own feelings towards the patient, and all of this helps you towards your own understanding. Now, when does the moment come, or how does the moment come, in which interpretation becomes possible? There's obviously a big disagreement, it seems to me, in psychoanalytic practice about when you intervene with interpretation. How do you deal with this issue, Jonathan Pedder?

Pedder: Well, I think that interpretation should be seen as just one form of intervention. I'm reminded of something Greenson said about different stages of intervention: confrontation, clarification, interpretation, working through. And there are many more kinds of things we do. You've talked about listening. And there are simply, human 'ah-has', grunts and encouraging noises and statements to invite someone to say more. And then one may be confronting somebody with a defensive attitude, seeking further clarification about a story or a dream or something they're telling, getting a clearer picture of it. So interpretation only comes after that.

Now, there may be people who say, maybe some of my colleagues will say, that the only significant interventions analysts make are interpretations. But I don't think that's the case. I think that's one special kind of intervention, when one tries to make sense of something the patient is saying both in the context of the relationship with oneself, the analyst, in the transference, and hopefully, in the most complete sense of interpretation, to then make some sense of it in relation to the past as well and to how you feel it originated.

Spillius: I wouldn't agree. I think the crux of it is getting one's understanding into an interpretation.

Ignatieff: What do you mean?

Spillius: Well, the thing about analysis, it's very peculiar, but basically it focuses a great deal on words. Words used expressively, but words used for communication. And that's part, a large part, of the point of the couch, as far as I'm concerned. It cuts down the cues. You know, the expressive movements and so on, so that neither analyst nor patient can see each other. And it means that a great deal of the expression has to be eventually translated into words, and into words that are comprehensible, that meet the patient's feeling, that don't go beyond what he can take at the time, but on the other hand are not just equivalent to a grunt. I remember one of my patients said to me once 'analysis by grunts is not enough'. I agreed with him. In other words the, you know, the expressions of sympathy are fine but they can be a cop-out for the analyst. Eventually I think one's got to move on.

Glasser: More fundamentally, I wonder whether we don't over-emphasise the importance of interpretation. I'll tell you what I'm getting at. I was thinking — I'd be interested to hear what you say about this — that analysis is rarely a process whereby the analyst helps the patient to create — I think of a work of art — create a sonata, let's say, which captures all the deepest and most profound emotions and attitudes and feelings, the inner soul of the patient. That captures it in the way a piece of art does. Which organises the content and adds cohesion and structure to it, which the patient comes with that somehow disorganised. And so what the aim of analysis is, is to help the patient to compose his own absolutely idiosyncratic sonata, not for public performance anyway, his own composition.

Pedder: I'd agree with that very much.

Glasser: And interpretation is just one of the ways of saying 'look, that discord you've put in there actually helps because it gives it a nice feeling of resolution there.' Or 'that discord's getting in the way.' Well that's an interpretation. But you might add some 'have you thought about putting in a C minor there, that does something.'

Ignatieff: But are you saying there that's what's wrong with patients is that they can't compose their own sonatas, and that you're there to help them to write a story or compose a story about their own lives that pulls fragments together?

Pedder: Very much. They can't write their own autobiography. I think Rycroft's talked about an analyst as an assistant biographer to the patient. That patients are unable to write their own sonata, their own story.

Ignatieff: Why not? It's a mysterious thought. I think we all have a commonsense sense that we can all write our autobiographies, but why can't they? Give me some examples, what do you mean?

Pedder: Because of emotional blocks, inhibitions, not being in touch with feelings within themselves, remote feelings from childhood. Can I just go back to add something to Mervyn's point because I very much agree with what he's saying about helping to write the sonata or the story, the autobiography for the patient? I think there's a common misunderstanding that interpretations are delivered *de haut en bas*, from the knowledgeable analyst who knows it all and tells the patient. I don't see it like that at all, as very much as Mervyn was saying, I think it is more of a joint work of art. A bit like Winnicott's squiggle game with children, where you do a drawing on a paper and the analyst does a squiggle and the child adds a squiggle and you see what you make of it together. I think that analysis is like that and making interpretations is like that. Somebody called it framing speculations as an invitation to mutual exploration. I think it's something like that. You're framing speculations, making a suggestion, could it be like this? And you're building up a picture between the two of you.

Ignatieff: But isn't this happy picture of a collaborative venture in the composition of autobiographies and sonatas just missing out resistance altogether, which is also fundamental to the analytical process?

Spillius: Indeed.

Ignatieff: That is, you give an interpretation and the patient says 'that's just rubbish as far as I'm concerned.' That it's much more a process of struggle than you're making it out.

Spillius: Oh yes, I find that. Especially at certain phases in an analysis. Towards the end, the description you have given, I think I would very much agree with. But there are terribly difficult times when that's not the case.

Glasser: Let's say we knew somehow that this piece, this passage in the sonata is absolutely wrong in some way. What we find is that a patient over and over again insists on writing that passage. And you might be able to very skilfully and with the patient's clear vision of it say 'look that's all wrong.' And they say 'yes it's all wrong.' And then a week later, or a month later, or a year later it's there.

Ignatieff: It comes back.
Glasser: It's there.
Ignatieff: But what do you do with resistance like that?
Glasser: Well the basic policy, as it were, is to try and understand what the resistance is about. In the old days, I think resistance was regarded as the enemy. You know, something which somehow or other's got to be broken or taken away from the patient. I think now we recognise that resistance is very much part of the patient's attempt to protect himself from pain and perhaps psychotic breakdown or something like that. And so, dealing with the resistance has to be something which is done very much in tune with where the patient is, what he can take. It's a very exciting process in a way because the two of you are working very carefully on a very delicate kind of operation.

Ignatieff: It's here I think that we get to the most mysterious part of your art which is the business of cure, the business of therapeutic benefit. I mean, it is deeply mysterious to many people that you can put two people in a room, that they can talk and listen to each other, that by simple processes of insight, empathy and understanding you can somehow unlock these neurotic blocks, these forgettings, these repressions and produce therapeutic benefit. How do you explain this process by which a process of talking becomes a process of cure and how does it happen?

Glasser: If you, the patient, find that you're kind of realising your potential, you're achieving, you're capable of functioning reasonably well, you're capable of coping with your shortcomings without expecting yourself not to have them, things like that I would think are a sign of a kind of coming togetherness, and I think it's one of the things that we and the patient and their friends feel. As a result of analysis, there's a certain sense of integration that comes across in a person's personality which I always find very encouraging.

Ignatieff: What do you mean by integration?
Glasser: That they hang together. That there's a certain harmony within themselves, a certain fluidity in the way they meet life. An elasticity, an adaptability I suppose is, I think, one of the key features. That they're capable of adapting to their internal circumstances and things that are going on inside themselves and the world around them.

Ignatieff: Insight, adaptability, hanging together. How do you think of cure?

Pedder: Well, can I just go back to when you said it's a deeply mysterious business that just talking about things should make people better? I was thinking about that, about the different historical phases in Freud's evolution of psychoanalysis as a method. Because there was the original cathartic method, merely talking about feelings, getting them off your chest, and that isn't mysterious is it? It's an ancient thing our idioms testify to: 'a problem shared is a problem halved,' and so forth. Getting things off your chest, the Catholic confession and so forth. That in itself is therapeutic, the catharsis.

Of course psychoanalysis developed into something else beyond that when things became re-enacted in the transference, in the relationship with the analyst. And there we move into this issue of integration, and Freud had different ways of talking about that, rather formal ways to begin with, like talking about 'making the unconscious conscious' and 'where id was there ego shall be' and so forth. But I think there's no better way of putting it than Rycroft did when quoting E.M. Forster, 'only connect the prose and the passion, live in fragments no longer, only connect and the monk and the beast which is in isolation, death to each other shall die...' Maybe I haven't got that quite right, but the idea that we need to undo inner splits, disintegrations and then warring parts of the personality come together I think is very much what analysis is about.

Ignatieff: How do you think of cure?

Spillius: I don't! I'd like to say one thing first which in a way is irrelevant to your question and that is that I think it's a very good idea when you're actually analysing not to think about cure or what's wrong or what would be better and so on. And Freud himself said this very, very vividly a long time ago and I was quite surprised to find it. He says, if I can read it, 'the most successful cases are those in which one proceeds, as it were, without any purpose in view, allows oneself to be taken by surprise by any new turn in them and always meets them with an open mind free from any presuppositions.' In other words, if you're thinking about cure, or almost any immediate practical aim, you're scuppered because your mind starts closing and you can't listen.

But having said that, I think after an analysis is over, or even in between sessions, it's very helpful to think 'right, what's going on?' and so on. Certain things change radically with some patients in analysis. A woman came with terrible depression and realised gradually that somehow, without knowing how it had happened, she wasn't depressed any more. Bad happenings would make her feel badly, but she didn't go into this *'mea culpa, mea culpa,* everything in the world is my fault' that she had. Now, other times I think one has to resign oneself as a patient to the fact that one's got difficulties, disabilities that one's going to have to live with and that it's no good thinking that these are all magically going to disappear.

Pedder: Cure's come to have a funny modern meaning: making whole or better and abolishing things through triumphs of modern surgery and antibiotics and things of that kind. Etymologically the word's the same root as to care for somebody — what the curate of souls does, or what we do curing bacon, you know, we're preserving it, caring for it. These all mean the same thing, so we don't hope to abolish all emotional difficulties. I like Freud's aphorism that analysis cannot do more than convert neurotic suffering into common human unhappiness. We're not attempting to abolish common human unhappiness, we're helping people to live with ordinary conflicts over human emotions.

Glasser: This has got a rather pessimistic feel to it which I don't like.

Ignatieff: You think we can do better?

Glasser: Well, I think so. Cure isn't the sort of cure you see in Hitchcock films where Gregory Peck realises what happened to him as a little boy and all's well, and I don't think a cure is the analyst talking a patient into what is healthy. I think it's much more helping the patient to realise their potential. It's much more a patient coming to terms with things inside himself which constrain him and restrict him and frustrate him and either he finds ways round them or he finds — I remember one of my trainers once put it very well, it was the time of the four minute mile, and he said often patients come to us as cripples and demand that we make them into four minute milers. Well, we don't seek to make them into four minute milers. Perhaps we can't save them from being a cripple, but we seek to help them to do very well as cripples, rather than to simply accept, 'well I'm a cripple.' That's a sort of pessimistic ring I didn't like. I think people can suffer from being too high-minded, demanding too much of themselves in terms of ideals and conscience and things like that, and coming to terms with that and living a freer, more expressive, more creative life is something that analysis can aim for without being pretentious and the golden answer.

Ignatieff: Now, let's turn to another issue that's terribly important, which is the actual interpretive discipline that you use to interpret and understand neurosis. Now, the Freudian theory, as I understand it, is that childhood experience, memories of childhood, childhood traumas and the normal passage of an infant through the Oedipus complex, the rearrangement of his relations with his mother and father, is a determining influence in adult neurosis. Now, I'm just wondering whether you could simply expound that theory of the determining effect of childhood experience and childhood memory on adult neurosis, because it's one of the most difficult aspects of Freudian theory to understand.

Spillius: I find this really difficult. And I think I know why. It's because we take it so much for granted that we don't think about it as something that needs explaining. Would you agree?

Pedder: But why is it such a puzzle? It isn't a specifically psychoanalytic idea, it's an idea in many other systems of thought. Don't the Jesuits say give them the child until they're five or seven and they're theirs for life or something?

Spillius: No, from the age of seven. And we're talking about what happens before.

Ignatieff: The age of two or three.

Spillius: And six months.

Pedder: Yes, but there are plenty of systems of thought that think that childhood years are determining. Ethological theories about imprinting in the early infancy of other animal species and so forth. There's nothing peculiar about psychoanalytic ideas that early infancy is a very important time in determining later character development.

Glasser: Isn't what is specific about the analytic emphasis on childhood the sort of things in childhood that we recognise and emphasise? And what has always reassured me about that is that if you work backwards from the patient, if you stick to the guideline that the patient must tell you what's there, rather than you know and you're just gonna get the patient to see it, you quite inevitably, invariably find that the way they are functioning is the result of things that have happened in childhood, of course. But what is found to be important are situations like the Oedipus triangle or earlier diadic relationships between mother and child, and that as you study what has happened, what's gone on, you see its influence on what the patient is doing with you in the transference, in his life. And so I think it's the clinical situation which leads you to the specific nature of what has happened in childhood that is relevant.

Ignatieff: (to Spillius) Now, the Kleinians, and you're a famous and important Kleinian, make an argument that is even more difficult for a layman to understand: that it's possible to trace back to really, really early infancy. You said 6 months, 18 months, two years. Now, convince me, as a sceptic, that analytical practice can actually get back to those stages, which seem to me so much behind the veil of any possible recovery. And that those really are determining influences on adult neurosis. Because it's a very hard thing for a layman to understand.

Spillius: Indeed it is. And especially things that happen before there are words are naturally very difficult to talk about directly and get themselves expressed, I think, in a continuing of what we call unconscious fantasy, which are always there and get corrected but still remain in the unconscious and get themselves expressed often very indirectly. Can I give an example, because it's difficult to generalise about this without going into a whole treatise about theory? I had a patient once who, in a consultation, was giving a perfectly coherent account of herself and in the middle of a sentence said 'hollow inside' and then continued her sentence as if she hadn't said it. So when she'd finished, I asked her: 'hollow inside?' And she looked very puzzled, so I said 'I thought you said hollow inside in the middle of your sentence.' And she said 'oh, did I?' And then she said 'well, I suppose I did,' and she went straight on with what she was talking about. Now, because it was a consultation and I don't make interpretations in consultations, and anyway I wasn't sure what it meant, I didn't say any more. But when her analysis began, it sounded just like any other analysis. She was giving all kinds of material that all made sense, about her parents being very busy people and wanting her to succeed and so on and so on, and I was making rather routine interpretations, everything was going fine. Except that as time went on I got very down and depressed and felt utterly futile, quite hopeless, all out of proportion to what was going on in the content of the analysis. I didn't know quite why I was feeling this or what I was picking up. And sometimes I would get very absent-minded and start thinking about other things and pull myself back and so on. Then gradually I decided that what was happening was that I was having 'hollow inside'. In other words, that I was having this experience of pointlessness, futility, uselessness, and she was being very effective and so on and wanting me to make good, sensible interpretations. And from that I got to the feeling that this was a repetition, in quite a subtle form, of a very early experience in which she felt that really she couldn't bring any experience of distress, meaninglessness, really acute anxiety, to her parents because what they wanted was a child who performed well and was everything nice, and one could not be miserable and hollow.

Ignatieff: That's a fascinating and even moving example. But how can you be sure that it traces back to one year old, to 18 months?

Spillius: I can't, but I'm pretty sure it traces back to before the time when she was facile with words, but that it's continued ever since, and that she can't say it. You know, she can say 'hollow inside' and she conveyed in her behaviour that hollow inside is not tolerated. You see, in other words she now does to herself what her parents, she feels, did to her. She dismisses hollow inside, at once, just a second of recognising it and then out it goes. She uses words to express it, I don't mean that people can't talk about it, but using words to express and communicate are not exactly the same.

Ignatieff: But almost the key theoretical scandal of Freudianism, if I can put it this bluntly, is the idea that psychic events, purely fantasised entities, can be as traumatic in their impact as real events. That is that the fantasy that you've been seduced can have as real effects on your psyche and later life as real events, as the actual experience of being seduced. And I still find that a very puzzling thought, and it must be very puzzling to your patients. How do you get that through to them, in a practical setting?

Glasser: Maybe we disagree on that, but in my opinion they're not the same.

Ignatieff: They're not the same?

Glasser: No, I think that the psychic event can have a powerfully traumatic and damaging effect and play a tremendously important role in adult neurosis. I don't question that. But that they are equivalent, you know, to take the question of childhood seduction, I think the impact of a real incestuous experience on a child is very different from a fantasy.

Pedder: And probably, sadly, much more common than one supposes.

Spillius: What is excruciating about it is that it — let us take a less extreme example, where a fantasy and the external reality work together, and this is a very common thing. I'm not thinking particularly of childhood seduction, where I think the shock of a total breaching of the parental role is so appalling that that takes precedent over one's own sexual wishes, infantile sexual wishes, and leads I think to a situation which it is really very difficult to live with for the rest of one's life. What I'm interested in too, is how do you tell the difference between an account that is imaginary and some representation of what really happened? And it's very difficult, I think.

Ignatieff: Good question. How do you? How do you answer your own question?

Spillius: Oh well, I thought the people who asked the questions didn't have to provide the answers. One thing I look for is consistency, over a long period of time. Not only about the particular story or episode but all the things surrounding it. And the other thing is that if I find that it has some kind of resonance in the transference of the moment, then I try and get it worked out in the transference, and often then see a change. For instance, if I can give an example — another one — quite a long time ago I had a patient, a man, who had an idea that his mother had, not seduced him, but that in early childhood she had been much more physical and had played with his penis and so on and got him very excited and then frustrated him. And I wondered is this so? Well, how does one tell? But at that time he was also trying to deal with really quite unruly sexual feelings about me which he thought were preposterous. You know, the falling in love with the analyst. And he was terribly embarrassed, thought it was ridiculous, etc, etc. Now, once we'd got through the thing in the transference, that I was seducing him by providing this opportunity to express himself, etc, etc, he no longer talked so much about what his mother had done in the bath and so on. Then many years later I reminded him of this and he said 'you know, I think that was totally untrue. Now that you mention it, I can remember saying it but I don't really think it was true.'

Consistency came into that. But I asked because I have always been interested in this, and also thinking of it for this programme too, I asked a colleague who works a lot with people who have been seduced in childhood what did he feel about this? And he said 'I think that usually in the account of someone who's actually had a very traumatic experience of this sort there is some detail of the environment that they remember.' And I suddenly thought 'ah-ha, I know what he means.' Can you remember what you were doing when Kennedy got shot? I think everybody can. I mean, that's not a sexual trauma. But in other words I think what we all do, and it comes from infancy, is when something awful is happening, you fix on something that will hold you together, some detail that you see. And since then, in thinking about it and checking it with other colleagues, they've remarked on the same thing. That is that somebody who's telling a story of an actual trauma will remember some utterly irrelevant environmental detail.

Ignatieff: Yes, we're moving towards a conclusion and it's appropriate therefore to talk about a question which is important in analysis, which is when do you terminate an analysis? You forge this very intense, often quite passionate, relationship in which the ego and the adult part is involved, and very childlike parts, as you said earlier. How is this relationship brought to an end? How do you terminate analysis, how does it work?

Pedder: I think there's something very like a mourning process goes on at the end of analysis. A separation, a mourning, and like in mourning where mourning goes right, eventually you're left with an internalisation of the person who's lost, and at the end of an analysis I think you're left with an internalisation of the analyst's analysing function. Somebody we ourselves can turn to in thinking over our own problems in the future.

Spillius: When things are getting ready to end, you know, most of the things that the person feels has troubled them are a bit better at least and they're more tolerant of themselves and more courageous about facing their difficulties, internal and external, something begins to happen. You find that in dreams or in odd references there are just scattered references to ending. And especially it tends to happen after some fairly dramatic improvement, there comes a feeling of 'this isn't going to last for ever,' and usually, if all is going well, with a feeling of sadness. In other words, a realisation that this relationship is not a way of life, it's something to help one live a life

and that weaning is beginning, is starting. They're very scattered at first, these references, and then gradually they consolidate, and then eventually one starts to think about when. And it usually is quite a moving and difficult and rather sad experience.
Ignatieff: For both of you?
Spillius: Yes, I think so.
Glasser: I think, in addition to the sort of things you were talking about, Elizabeth, there are certain criteria patient and analyst can use. Such as observing that they are functioning better, that they're handling their life better, that they're coping better, that they're more flexible, that they are realising their potential. The sadder side of it is that termination may be due to the fact that the analysis is not getting anywhere or is kind of stuck.
Ignatieff: How do you know that when it happens?
Glasser: Well, exactly that. You, patient and analyst, work away at things and find that nothing really has changed. In the patient, not in the outside world so much as within the patient, within the sessions themself.
Spillius: But I think in a sense a good analyst doesn't end. What I mean by that is that the patient takes away with him not an analyst or a memory of an analyst but a process, a function, an understanding of how to face things. I don't mean that they sit down and analyse themselves every day, but they have new capacities for coping with their own anxieties, defences, external situations, and in times of difficulty can sit down and think 'now, what's this about?'
Ignatieff: We've come to the end of our programme with this descent into the strange world of the analytical session. I think we understand a little more clearly now why it's an impossible profession. It's not merely listening to and trying to help people who are often disturbed, often confused, often speaking a language which is very hard to understand. It's also a difficult profession because you have to know yourself, the Socratic injunction 'know thyself' is joined in psychoanalysis to that other injunction: 'physician, heal thyself.'

Chapter 3

Psychoanalysis: Truth or Science?

Michael Ignatieff
with Adolf Grünbaum, André Green
and Robert Young

Ignatieff: Let's begin with a story. A patient whose father had died of a drink-damaged liver told his analyst about a dream. In the dream he meets his father and gives him a bunch of flowers: six roses. 'Six roses or cirrhosis?' the analyst asks. What are we to make of this? Is the analyst *right*? Has his intervention got to the *truth* of the matter? And how does he *know* he's right? For years a fierce debate has been going on about just these questions. To critics of psychoanalysis, such a tenuous link between six roses and cirrhosis seems a long way away from the serious world of hard science. And yet Freud himself began as a brilliant scientist and always insisted on the truth of his ideas. Behind the debate on psychoanalysis and truth stands the question of *cure*. How do analysts back up their claims to cure personal suffering and distress? What makes one of their interpretations more true than another? Finally, how useful is the language of science itself as a way of understanding our innermost feelings?

With me tonight to discuss these questions are Adolf Grünbaum, American philosopher of science and author of *The Foundations of Psychoanalysis: A Philosophical Critique*; André Green, one of France's most eminent psychoanalysts and author of the recently published collection of essays *On Private Madness*; and Robert Young, critic of science and editor of *Free Associations*, a journal on psychoanalysis and culture.

Adolf Grünbaum, let me begin with you. Are you saying that psychoanalysis has simply no claims to scientific truth?

Grünbaum: No, that would be much too strong. It seems to me that what we have to do is to look at the major claims that psychoanalytic theory has made about various areas of human behaviour. One, the development of disorders of specified sorts; two, the production of dreams; three, the production or commission of various slips of the tongue, the mishearings, misspeakings, misplacings etc, generally speaking, bungled actions. The main claims that psychoanalytic theory has made about these phenomena was to offer causal explanations of them, to pick out presumed causal factors which are held to be explanatory of the occurence of these phenomena.

One of the major methods psychoanalytic theory has used to validate its claims is the method of free association: a method which Freud pioneered after he abandoned the use of hypnosis that had been employed by other people such as Breuer, his senior mentor. And as I see it, the heart of the use of free association as a method of validating causal claims is the following: that if a patient takes a symptom of his own or her own and then freely associates to it and after a while a repressed thought emerges, then, according to the theory, *that* factor, *that* repression, can be held to have been a contributory causal factor to the formation of the given phenomenon, be it the symptom, be it a dream, or a particular dream element, or the commission of a slip, such as misspeaking or a mishearing.

In my view, this method cannot in fact validate the causal claims that it makes. In order to validate these causal claims, other methods of inquiry seem to me to be necessary. And that seems to me to be the heart of the critique of psychoanalytic theory as a theory of human nature. Of course it also is a therapy. However, its major influence in Western culture, to my knowledge, has been as a theory of human nature, because only a tiny fraction of the population undergoes long-term psychoanalysis, and while, of course, as therapy it is also important — and much needs to be said about that — its major intellectual impact has been as a theory of human nature.

Ignatieff: Okay. A lot to unpack there. As a practising analyst, André Green, do you have an initial reaction to this criticism?

Green: Lots of reactions.

Ignatieff: Lots of reactions. The more the better.

Green: Ah, beware. Psychoanalysis is not interested in human behaviour. You will not find that it is a concern of psychoanalysts. Psychoanalysts as *psycho*-analysis means, are interested in the analysis of human psyche. Now to focus on the criticism of free association one has first to understand what free association is, and what is the actual view about free association. In Freud's mind, the free association method was a procedure, I would even say an artefact, if you wish, because free association doesn't exist in the ordinary exchanges between people. So he introduced a new way of having the ability to have access to a spontaneous work of the mind, and this is the paradox of the analytic situation, which looks like no other situation. One is asked to talk as if one was alone in the presence of someone who is there and is in fact not there because he doesn't engage in a dialogue with the person who talks. And this situation, talking as if you were talking to yourself when you're alone, in the presence of someone else who is absent, is a totally new situation.

Now, when Freud asks for free association, there is a very naive understanding of it that would think that Freud was looking for confessions, that people had some dirty things to say that they wouldn't dare to say, and that they could say to this very special person which was the psychoanalyst. But in a later work, Freud insisted on the fact — well maybe he did not express it — that it was not only a removal of the moral censorship, but of the *intellectual* censorship. It was a device to put in parenthesis for one hour a day our usual ways of reasoning when we are with other people in discussion, the intellectual removal of censorship. And when an analyst gives the fundamental rule to an analysand before starting the analysis he doesn't ask him to confess his sins, he says 'say whatever comes to your mind, even if it seems *meaningless*.'

So this is a way of functioning, and I disagree with what Adolf Grünbaum just said about if you ask a patient to take a symptom and free associate on this symptom, *no* analyst will ever do that today. What he will ask is for free association at every session, the patient being in a position to talk about anything which comes to his mind. I would even say that an analyst would consider it a resistance if the analysand takes the symptom as such and tries to free associate on that symptom. Now, one thing to end with these preliminary remarks, Adolf Grünbaum's remarks are valid for the attempts made by Freud in 1895.

Ignatieff: A long time ago.

Green: Ninety years. Today, we have new conceptions, which include free associations in a larger concept, which is the concept of the setting, which was invented by someone from this country, Winnicott, who understood the importance of the setting.

Ignatieff: The analytic setting?

Green: Yes, the analytic setting. To speak today of the free association method without including it in its more general procedure, which is the setting, is today a rather retarded way of thinking about psychoanalysis. Now, what is the justification of the setting and the free association method? It is the attempt to recreate the model of the dream and to disentangle the language from reason, logical reason, logical thought, and this disentanglement, it's like if you take your pullover and pull on it, you see the holes, you see the network. When you look at it it seems united, in fact it is a network. And in this network you pick up or you point up your six roses — cirrhosis. You should have said that the example is in French, in that in French *six roses*, six roses, and *cirrhose*, cirrhosis, is a case of total homophony, which is a very important problem for linguists.

Ignatieff: Yes, that was one of the most interesting and persuasive discussions of free association I think I've ever heard, and very valuable. (to Grünbaum) I can sense, even without looking at you, that you're champing at the bit to come back, but I'd like to ask Bob Young to comment on this. Where are we at this point, in your view?

Young: Well I've been sitting here doing something which the Reichian calls 'pulsing', in the sense that the frame of reference of our discussion seems to move very quickly back and forth between a quite precise discussion about testability in a clinical setting, and an attempt, if I've understood André Green's impatience correctly, to say 'it's not like that, it's a *process* and we actually have to see it as a process and we don't heap up single facts and put them on the shelf and say "true or false?" in the way that we might in a laboratory discovery, or even a fact in everyday life.' That is, it is an ongoing set of interactions with a lot of silence and a lot of tolerance and a lot of ability to test. Now, if we do try to reduce it to criteria appropriate to the philosophy of science, I think we do a disservice to truth, but I think we also, if we try to reduce it to Freud, do a disservice to psychoanalysis.

Ignatieff: What disservice to psychoanalysis? I didn't follow the last point?

Young: Freud died on the eve of World War Two and hasn't written a word since. And, as André Green said, the whole question of the interaction, not only the transference — that is, what the patient projects onto the analyst — but what the analyst experiences inside and may or may not choose to communicate, or may wait 6 months or 18 months to communicate — that is, the counter-transference — has been investigated very carefully indeed, and there's a whole literature on it. There's also a whole set of debates about what are the appropriate criteria for acting in certain ways. Psychoanalysis is not an Old Testament set of tablets written in stone, it's an evolving process.

Ignatieff: And are you implying there that in a sense Adolf Grünbaum is taking a kind of old canonical Freud as if the tradition hadn't moved, and it has moved?

Young: Not only has it moved in the psychoanalysis of adults, it's moved in the psychoanalysis of children very dramatically in this country with the work of both Anna Freud and Melanie Klein, and indeed a third person, Margaret Lowenfeld who worked on this matter. It isn't inferring what happened in the past, it's actually looking at the progress of the child's experiences. But I was trying to make two points at once. One of them had to do with 'let us broaden our conception of what we mean by psychoanalysis,' but let us also broaden our conception about what we mean by, if I understand the title correctly, science versus truth. We believe there is some tension between testability as a criterion appropriate to natural science, or indeed the natural science claims which Freud did indeed make about psychoanalysis, on the one hand, and what convinces us that something is true on the other. And this is a much broader question. Not a question which we can settle only in the setting of the analytic encounter.

Ignatieff: I want to put Adolf Grünbaum out of his misery. You're being accused, to summarise you grossly, of misunderstanding free association, misunderstanding the analytical situation fundamentally. And what's your reply to that?

Grünbaum: Well, I would like to put it into a somewhat wider context, if I may, because Dr Green said a number of things. There is the charge of anachronism, there is the charge of misunderstanding what goes on in the transaction, there is the charge that psychoanalysis has become a very different sort of thing. What I would like to understand is, whatever the method is that is used as Dr Green uses it — and of course I don't profess to know what he does with his patients, I only can read what descriptions I find about the methods that are used — I would like to know on the strength of what an analyst claims to know what produced a patient's current life problems? Why a patient dreamt what he did? Why a person misspeaks himself or herself? Or even why somebody finds certain things funny? This is what I would like to know. And if the method as I described it is a schematisation, well and good. I would like to know how the methods that are in fact used as more sophisticated versions of this deliver what they claim to deliver. How do analysts in fact, in the clinical setting, in the treatment transaction, certify certain occurrences as having been causally relevant?

With respect to the charge of anachronism, there are two things I would like to say. First of all, I have found Freud's own arguments incredibly more ingenious and more brilliant than some of the arguments given by his later exponents. If I'm told that the theory has changed, I would like to know what the current theory is, because obviously there is an enormous range of hypotheses among analysts, and I would like to know from any one particular school on what grounds the claims that they now claim they make in lieu of those that Freud made are in fact held to be valid.

Ignatieff: There's so many questions there, so many issues, I think we ought to unpack them. And your use of the word *cause* and the question of cause, I think, is a good place to start. And let's make this as simple as we can. A man comes to an analyst with a phobia about rats, analysis uncovers or reveals unpleasant memories of rats, fantasies about rats, experiences with rats in childhood. Now, it seems to me the question you're asking is 'do the memories, trauma or fantasies, cause the phobia, what entitles an analyst to say that there's a causal relationship between the material produced in analysis and the phobia itself?' And as a practising analyst, how do you deal with this question of cause, that you're being addressed with by Adolf Grünbaum?

Green: I can't take this case in detail, because that would completely take all the time for the discussion. But I'll come to your example, because I know what you're talking about, because the writer who gave that example is one of my friends. Of course you say what is the relationship between six roses and cirrhosis? Well, this is what we call a clinical vignette. I have reservations about clinical vignettes, but it's just an example to see how in language and through the defences of language some content which belongs to the unconscious can be shown. What are the hypotheses behind it? This man has lost his father from alcoholism. He undergoes an analysis with an analyst. There is a process — and this is the basic hypothesis of psychoanalysis — of transference. In that dream, that patient displays a feminine attitude towards his analyst. He wants to seduce the analyst. Or you can say it's a very eroticised situation. The analyst's assumption in such a case is that behind such an apparent seductive, *loving* attitude there are ambivalent feelings which conceal a certain *hostility*. The fact that the analyst associates between *six roses* and *cirrhose* — I say it in French because it's obvious — the analyst picks this point up from the *previous* material. It doesn't fall from heaven. It comes from all the previous sessions in which the analyst has witnessed the extreme ambivalent or hostile feelings towards the father. So he gives the and be a good analysand and full of loving feelings, and he knows from the history of the past that this patient has repressed the ambivalent or hostile feelings towards his father. So he gives the interpretation in terms of a play on words based on homophony. He doesn't say to the patient, 'now we've got the key, we know what happened, we have the cause and tomorrow you'll be cured and the analysis will end.' It's just one moment in the analysis. The analyst gives the interpretation, he doesn't *impose* the interpretation. And he sees what comes after. It may be that the material will not confirm the hypothesis of that ambivalence, either because it is too repressed or maybe the analyst is wrong.

Ignatieff: But it seems to me Adolf Grünbaum's questions still remain relevant. Which is that, if certain scientific status has been asserted for psychoanalysis, not only by its founders but by a whole tradition, and not merely by its American, vulgar proponents, if psychoanalysis is claimed to be a science, what are we to make of that claim? Are you simply saying 'that's an irrelevant claim, a historically outmoded one, it's a red herring, we're a different kind of discipline, a much more interactive discipline,' I mean, what is psychoanalysis?

Green: I do not say that at all.

Ignatieff: What would you say?

Green: I'd reverse the question.

Young: Excellent!

Green: Let's take the criteria for truth in logic, even the Popperian ones, why not? And let's take the criteria of science, and let's ask ourselves what is the applicability of these criteria? What is their usefulness for ordinary lives? Take your life, 24 hours a day, think of what you've done, said, felt, in terms of love, hate, disappointment, anxiety, success, joy, all that happened in yourself, and try to apply these criteria in terms of truth or falseness. What is the result? Total failure. I ask a question to Professor Grünbaum: when you look at a Rembrandt self portrait in terms of true or false, what is your conclusion? When you hear a Shakespeare play in terms of true or false, what is your conclusion? When you hear a Johann Sebastian Bach mass, what is your conclusion in terms of true or false?

Grünbaum: The answers are very different in different contexts. If I say 'oh, what a beautiful day,' in expressing joy, I'm not concerned with any beliefs or claims and with assessing them. And in order to talk about Shakespeare I would say that in my view one of the reasons that Shakespeare has been so fantastically influential and has delighted generations of people is that he seems to put his finger on things that ring true and he said them beautifully.

Ignatieff: But what about Freud?

Grünbaum: I'm coming to that. Whether the things that ring true are in fact well-founded, that of course is the question. And here I want to come to what I believe is a red herring all the way, and that has to do with the misdepiction of my attitudes. First of all, if I didn't recognise Dr Taylor's point that psychoanalytic theory has been very influential in culture I wouldn't have worked very hard to examine it.

Young: Can we comment on this Freudian slip please?

Grünbaum: Excuse me?

Young: It's all right, never mind, carry on, not amusing.

Grünbaum: I'm not in the business of flogging dead horses.

Young: I'm not in the business of being Dr Taylor either, but go ahead.

Grünbaum: I beg your pardon.

Young: It's all right.

Grünbaum: Now, the — Dr Young, I'm sorry.

Young: It was meant as a joke about Freudian slips, if you don't mind.

Grünbaum: No, that's fair game. No, that's fine. I would like to say another thing about my appreciation of psychoanalytic theory. In fact, in a review symposium of my book that appeared in the June 1986 issue of the *Journal of the Behavioural and Brain Sciences* I wrote the following: 'I find some empirical plausibility in the psychoanalytic theory of defence mechanisms. For example, denial and rationalisation, reaction formation, projection and identification.' This is not the same as to say that the etiological theories of psychoanalysis are well-founded in my view.

Ignatieff: What do you mean by etiological theories?

Grünbaum: The theories about the causes or origins of human disorders, such as obsessive, compulsive disorder. And that brings me to the term 'causal' and causation. Freud early on, in 1895, gave a magnificent typology of different sorts of causes and causally relevant factors. And I would like to give an example of what I have in mind and what I think is faithful to his typology of causes, and give a very concrete example, deliberately chosen from the field of medicine rather than the field of psychology, of psychotherapy. Take the claim that syphilis is the only cause of paresis.

Ignatieff: What's paresis? I know what syphilis is.

Grünbaum: Paresis is an advanced stage of syphilis, tertiary syphilis, in which there are fundamental breakdowns of the nervous system. Dr Green is a doctor, he could say much more about this.

Now, when somebody says that syphilis is the only cause of paresis, we have to realise that the majority of untreated syphilitics do not in fact become paretics, that is aren't afflicted by this, only a minority do. And yet one says that syphilis, that is untreated syphilis, is the only cause of paresis. And what I think is going on here and in many other cases of causation is the following: let's take the class of syphilitics and divide them into two sub-classes, those that are treated and those that are untreated. Then we will find that there is a higher incidence of paresis among those that are untreated than among those that are treated. Indeed, since syphilis — untreated syphilis — is the only cause of paresis, you will never find a paretic who was not also a syphilitic. Now, that is a much more sophisticated notion of being a causal factor than the ones that are often talked about.

What I would submit is that when I talk about wanting to have validation of psychoanalytic claims, what I'm asking for is validation of causal claims in this much more refined sense, which are made and which Freud explained very, very carefully in his typology of causes. Freud talked about cases in which certain antecedents were causally necessary. That is, if you didn't have them you wouldn't have the outcome. There were other cases in which they were not causally necessary, and he distinguished between them.

Finally, on the matter of demanding testability and scientificity, I would be perfectly happy to drop the use of the word science altogether and simply to ask on what grounds these claims are made, why we should accept them rather than other claims? If you ask me why I like Shakespeare better than some very poor writer I can tell you, but I don't think the answer to that bears on the question of whether any of the explanations that are offered either by Freud or by neo-Freudians, or by Dr Green or anyone else, why anyone should accept them rather than reject them. And so I think the issue of testability has been, I think, misrepresented.

Young: We should accept them because they resonate with the dialectic of experience.

Ignatieff: What do you mean by the dialectic of experience, for God's sake?

Young: I was going to explain, thank you, Michael. Because there are definitions of truth that seem to me don't conform to that, I'm sorry to say, tedious example we've just had. Because truth actually has to do with resonances. It has to do with whether or not something touches someone else, it has to do with whether or not it causes them to feel in rapport with what's been said. I'm using these terms very loosely and very deliberately, because I do think truth in the larger sense is one of the terms our discussion tonight is about.

Richard Rorty speaks of Freud as showing us that each person is 'a creator of metaphors,' and he calls truth 'a moving army of metaphors.' I would find it impossible, although I'm prepared to be proven wrong, to square that rhetoric with the rhetoric of the example of paresis we've just had. It's a different way of speaking about experience, a different way of speaking about truth. I do not wish to throw out of the window testability, verifiability, causality etc, I don't want to do that at all. But I would like for all of us to acknowledge, and in particular Professor Grünbaum, that there is a large movement in the philosophy of science which is now saying that truth is *made* not found, that it's socially constructed, that we have to see it in the same way we speak about Shakespeare and art and music and so forth and that there isn't the kind of accountability.

In the 1950s, an example like the one that was given about paresis would have gone without protest, it would have been seen as the norm, it would have been seen as legitimate. I was a student in this period, and in fact the example you started with, of where I say 'it's a beautiful day,' I was walking down the street with my Professor at Yale and we walked up to Arthur Papp, a logical positivist and we said 'Isn't it a beautiful day Arthur?' And do you know what Arthur said: 'I presume you're speaking metaphorically.' And it wasn't relevant.

Grünbaum: I'm not responsible for that.

Young: No, what I would say is there's an incommensurability between concepts of how we find truth here.

Green: Professor Grünbaum's example about general paresis draws us back to the early 19th century.

Grünbaum: That's all right.

Green: The concept of causality now cannot be raised in such simple terms as you raise it.

Grünbaum: May I comment on that?

Green: No, I'm sorry. Because I think that the trouble with Professor Grünbaum is that he's shifted from physics to psychoanalysis and maybe he still thinks in terms of the rationality which comes into play in the physical world, which means in the non-living world, and tries to apply them to the psychical world. Now, in terms of etiology I want to say Freud never denied that there could be a biological etiology. Myself, I cannot think of any mental state, normal or abnormal, which is not rooted in brain activity. I think I would be stupid if I were to say that the conversation I am having is not involving my brain mechanism. This is not the point. The point is to try to specify the peculiarity, the originality of what has to be called psychic causality.

Ignatieff: A brief come-back on this point.

Grünbaum: First of all, the objection to the old 19th century view seems to operate, to me, with a caricature of the 19th century view. Freud was perfectly explicit, he used the example of tuberculosis to point out that the tubercle bacillus is not a sufficient cause for tuberculosis. Lots of people carry tubercle bacilli, they don't become tubercular. The next thing is I want to make clear that I use the example of syphilis and paresis only to give a concrete example of how a factor can be causally relevant without saying anything at all about the role of physiologic or other factors in psychic causation. The claim that untreated syphilis is causally relevant to paresis here is the claim that the probability of paresis in these two sub-classes is different. This, I submit, can be applied to all kinds of other statements about factors being causally relevant to outcome. It is neutral as between whether these factors are psychic or not.

Ignatieff: But are you answering the question that there are simply different truth criteria at work in the psychic realities that we're discussing? Because that's the heart of Bob Young's point.

Grünbaum: I would like to comment on that. I hope it's a fair question to ask you, how you would respond to somebody who says it 'coheres with his experience' to believe some of the doctrines the Nazis put forward? After all, if we have all kinds of different kinds of truth, and if they are just coherent with experience in some unspecified way, how are you going to distinguish between theories that you would, I hope, consider in some respects to be clearly false, theories that make certain claims about racial causation of various traits and behaviours? Aren't you opening the door to anything and everything?

When you talk about the business of different species of truth, I should have thought that we have to distinguish first of all between perhaps different modes of validation without thereby automatically claiming that to ascribe truth to the claims is a different thing in the one case from the other. I would submit that it may well be possible that in different contexts validation may take different forms and have different methods, although that has to be argued for and cannot merely be asserted authoritatively. But the attribution of truth itself, it seems to me, is not different if we say that something is true about the human psyche or if we say that something is true about who committed a murder, or if we say that something is true about why a person dreamt.

Young: Yes, I want to answer that. I think a child brought up in Nazi Germany, who was born, shall we say, in 1935 and reached the age of 10 in 1945, the truth of that child's experience would be Nazism, probably, unless it was Jews hidden in a concentration camp in a certain sub-culture. That would be the truth of that child's experience, and the problem in 1945, as we all know, and who's to say it's finished, was to deal with that fact. I spoke to a group of Argentinian refugees who live in Mexico, who go to Nicaragua, and the first group of children they were asked to treat, as psychoanalysts, was 100 boys under the age of 10 who had been taught to remove the eyes of people. And their fathers had gone off to fight with the Contras. The truth of those children's experience is that they get security from being sadists.

Grünbaum: No one denies that people who are conditioned to believe certain particular things in a culture, or privately, will believe that these claims are true. It is a fact that people who are conditioned to believe certain claims, if they learn the use of the term 'true', they will then believe them to be true.

Ignatieff: That does not make them true.

Grünbaum: The fact that doesn't show anything about whether they are true and the fact that there is an enormous cultural diversity in what people take their experience to betoken doesn't show at all that all of these incompatible things are true, or for that matter that any of them are true. So I am with you in the recognition of the potency of the cultural influences, the fundamental role they play in the very conceptualisations that people have. But that, so far as I can see, does nothing to undermine either the idea that it's clear what we understand by saying that a statement is true, or that it's at least to some extent clear. And secondly, that we can discuss under what circumstances a person is entitled to attribute this property to a belief or a system of beliefs or to claims that are made in other contexts.

Young: I stand corrected, and I apologise. I shot myself in the foot that time. What I should have said was that truth doesn't make a damn bit of difference in that context. If you separate truth from the moral, ideological, political and historical dimensions of the example of children in Nazi Germany. And one of the things that's happening in the philosophy of science these days is that people are turning *to* psychoanalysis rather than having a go at it, to say that there is something about psychoanalytic discourse that has something to teach to the philosophy of science.

Now here I can draw briefly on my own experience. Briefly, I promise you. And that is, if we do look closely at, shall we say, Newton, which people have looked at very carefully in this way, Darwin, whom I've looked at carefully in this way, and look at the hearts of their theories, we do not find things that correspond to these astringent conceptions of testability, validity, truth, falsifiability, whatever hard-nosed criterion you want to erect. We find at the heart of Darwin's theory an anthropomorphic metaphor replete with teleology. That is, with purposive explanation connected to human intentions. We find at the heart of Newton a mysticism, a hermeticism. Somebody once said to try to bring mathematical criteria to bear on understanding who Newton was and what Newton's truth was is like using a spanner — or a wrench in America — to mend a sock. It's just not an appropriate dissecting tool for looking at it.

And part of my impatience, and I'm sorry if it descends to rudeness sometimes, is that I keep wanting to say 'What does Grünbaum think about human nature? What's going on here?' I'm not trying to diagnose you. I'm just saying 'Come on man, tell me what you really think about human nature, will you?' Because I don't think this stuff about falsifiability or testability is very interesting.

Ignatieff: But let me toss it back at you, Bob Young. If you find at the heart of Darwinism an anthropomorphism joined to a teleology, what do you find at the heart of psychoanalysis? I mean, specifically what do you make of the metaphor of science, constantly deployed?

Young: Two things to say. One of them is, let us not have more stringent criteria for psychoanalysis than we do for other forms of investigation. Especially I do think Darwin and Newton are sort of up there with the goodies in the scientific canon. And the second thing is — I wasn't being facetious or merely trying to turn the tables when I said people are looking to psychoanalysis rather than having a go at it, because, and here I'm drawing on aspects of Habermas, not all of them, they are saying it has a reflexive quality, it has a quality where the interactions are clear, something which comes from the phenomenological tradition which says 'we don't have subjects and objects, we have I's and thou's.' That is, there is always in the other something which is in contact with us.

And the way the philosophy of science, or the philosophy of science in this style, speaks to psychoanalysis is to say, let us try to retain the sort of distinction between the knowing subject and the known object and the gap between them which is associated with the mind-body problem, with the subject-object distinction in traditional philosophy, which is in dead trouble, with the primary-secondary quality distinction between things that are hard and mathematical and things that are subjective like colours, odours and taste. Now a lot that's going on in the philosophy of science has to do with transcending these stark and sharp distinctions and saying experience isn't like that, interpersonal relations aren't like that, and truths, including scientific truths, aren't like that.

And by the way, why throw up these criteria that aren't met by physics itself? So what I would say about the metaphor of science is that it's a form sometimes — and here I would not accuse you of this — of conceptual terrorism, to say 'you don't meet this criterion, you don't meet this criterion, you don't meet this criterion, it's nonsense.'

Grünbaum: I would like to know what criteria are applicable and why and how rival claims are adjudicated. If I could hear once this evening how rival claims that are each said to be authenticated by these non-validational methods, that is methods other than the ones that are being attributed to me, rightly or wrongly, I would like to know how that's done.

Ignatieff: Let's address these.

Young: Truth to experience in the process of the analysis itself, borne out or not by subsequent life. And I would say, by the way, it's also true of psychoanalysis or psychotherapy.

Ignatieff: How borne out by subsequent life? You're saying subsequent life is in a sense the test.

Young: I'll tell you something even stronger than this, and I'm sure Dr Green will bear me out. If a patient comes with a distressing symptom, and in the course, especially in the early course of the analysis, that symptom disappears, the criterion will not be whether the symptom is there or not. The criterion will be whether in the transference there's a change. Because there's flight into health, there's acting out, there are all sorts of ways people can change behaviourally, that bear no relationship to the underlying process. Only what happens finally and fundamentally in the transference and the quality of the subsequent experience — and I do not now mean the behaviour or the presence or the absence. And indeed, in conditioning therapy the simpler things are chosen that can be persuaded away. I mean, while we're being rude about persuasion, what on earth is conditioning therapy except very coercive persuasion?

Ignatieff: Somebody listening, perhaps not as carefully as they should, would say that what you've just said makes it appear that the proof of psychoanalytic efficacy depends on changed relations between the patient and the analyst.

Young: I'm sorry, I do think that. Why is that imprecise listening?

Ignatieff: But surely that would potentially give a grotesque result. That is, his behaviour towards the analyst is changed, what about the rest of his life?

Green: It's not a problem of behaviour. Again, again and again.

Young: Let me answer the question, because I've been asked it, then if you wish to comment on it, please do. Michael, the relationship, which is sometimes the most intimate relationship that a person has in their life, especially if they've had very damaged relations in their early life, it is a second chance, a chance to reconstruct one's primary relations — they're called object relations, but relations with significant people — the quality of that, which really is only known between those two people, is the touchstone, the final test. I know I'm playing into Professor Grünbaum's hands for saying this, but it's the simple truth.

Ignatieff: Yes, but does André Green agree with that?

Young: I think he does.

Green: I do agree, but I would like to add something. Professor Grünbaum has the feeling that we're trying to escape his crucial questions. I don't want to escape your crucial questions. What I say is that you are asking your question from a certain point of view which is yours and that you ask us to come in and to submit to this point of view, this point of view having the criteria for the distinction between truth and falsibility.

Ignatieff: We're coming right to the end of this discussion, so you're going to have to summarise very quickly.

Green: My conclusion would be the following: if truth is what is described by science, then I think that psychoanalysis is not scientific, though I think it is true. And my conclusion is that the models of science, when applied to the human mind, have to be rethought. Lacan defines psychoanalysis as one member of a family of what he called *Les Sciences Conjecturales*, conjectural sciences. When we look at another modern thinker of psychoanalysis — I mean Bion — Bion considered that we had to add to the two great main axes for understanding the human mind, love and hate, a third parameter, which he called knowledge. Science was in his view one vertix of knowledge. And I think I agree with what he said.

Winnicott introduced us to the importance of considering the paradoxes, as a logical form to understand psychic activity. I think that in the future the logic of the unconscious will develop and extend considerably. I think that Freud has only initiated the problem. Freud wrote the alphabet, but now we have to learn to read foreign texts in other languages. Because we can see from our experience that the logic of neurosis is not the logic of depression, is not the logic of psychosis, is not the logic of psychosomatics. There are different types of logic, though all have their roots in the unconscious.

And I think that the more psychoanalysis will develop, the more the analyst will have to learn to think in terms of what I have called 'private madness.' People who are normal, who have ordinary lives, families, social responsibilities, but who show their private madness on the couch. Unless the analyst is trained to that new way of thinking and is able himself to think in terms of the logic of the patient in these different fields, analysis will not progress.

Ignatieff: Now, the question to you, Professor Grünbaum is slightly different. You've made some very trenchant, much rebutted criticisms of psychoanalysis this evening. Put crudely, if psychoanalysis doesn't work, what forms of knowledge about the human self, about the human predicament, are we going to have to develop to do better?

Grünbaum: Well, let me put that in context if I may, and, as Dr Green mentioned earlier, my perspective is of course primarily an American one in so far as psychoanalysis is an institution in addition to being a theory. In the United States at least there is a major crisis in psychoanalysis. The number of young people, the candidates who enter psychoanalytic training is declining massively. Furthermore, there is pressure from insurance companies and third part reimbursers to give evidence that the therapy does some of the things that people expect when they enter therapy. And there are at least two quite different responses to that situation in the psychoanalytic community in the United States. Of course there are others, but let me single out the two that seem to me to be important in relation to the question you posed. One is to me a self-defeating one, and that is to draw the wagons in a circle and to say that the challenge comes from an external perspective and that it isn't asked from the inside. Of course, almost any challenge against a theory comes in a certain sense from an external perspective, because if you stay inside the theory and accept it there'd be no reason to ever get out. Now, the other response to that crisis is to join up the rest of the intellectual community, and I mean here not the entire intellectual community necessarily, but that part of the intellectual community that is interested in testing hypotheses, not in any crude sense, but in the way in which, say, cognitive psychologists test their hypotheses, and to say we must make common cause with these people and we must do so of course in a sophisticated way. So I would like to make common cause with that segment of the psychoanalytic community in the United States and elsewhere that does want to endorse the use of various methods of validation that are familiar from their earlier inquiries, that are being used by cognitive psychologists and other people who want to know why they should give credence to, use, apply, adhere to, apply in the human and other areas in the humanities, the brilliant hypotheses which form the Freudian legacy.

Ignatieff: We're going to have to stop right here. You've been listening to a debate, passionate and intense. I hope you understand from listening to it why psychoanalysis is at the very heart of our culture, why it's at the very heart of our passionate struggle to know and understand ourselves.

CHAPTER 4

Psychoanalysis: What Do Women Want?

Michael Ignatieff with
Janine Chasseguet-Smirgel, Jean Baker Miller
and Juliet Mitchell

Ignatieff: In her book *The Second Sex*, Simone de Beauvoir wrote 'one is not born but rather becomes a woman.' This leads right to the heart of one of the most exciting debates in recent years: how does a baby girl become a woman? Is it all a matter of anatomy and biology, the maternal instinct? Or do we acquire our gender, our innermost feelings and desires? One of the most controversial figures in this whole debate of course is Freud. Through the sixties and early seventies he came under heavy attack from feminists for his notorious theories about penis envy, and for seeming to argue that women are naturally passive, even inferior. Freud's writings, they said, were simply part of his time, another fossil of late Victorian patriarchy. His attempt to talk about women in terms of their nature and biology were simply wrong. But others have pointed out that Freud was one of the first doctors to actually listen to his women patients, and that psychoanalysis, through the work of Karen Horney, Anna Freud and Melanie Klein, has been one area of our culture where women have been able to define and explore their gender. According to this view, psychoanalysis has been pointing to new ways of thinking about how women become what they are.

With me tonight to discuss these issues are Jean Baker Miller, American psychotherapist, feminist and author of *Towards a New Psychology of Women*; Janine Chasseguet-Smirgel, French psychoanalyst and editor of *Female Sexuality*, one of the first books to raise these issues within psychoanalysis; and Juliet Mitchell, well-known feminist and psychoanalyst, author of *Psychoanalysis and Feminism*, *Women, the Longest Revolution*, and most recently editor of the selected writings of Melanie Klein.

Jean Baker Miller, I thought I'd begin with you. You've had 20 years of experience treating women in a clinical setting. What do you think Freud got right in his thinking about femininity and what do you think is missing or incomplete in his account?

Miller: Well, let me start with what I consider the very basic contributions of Freud, which have everything to do with women, but also men. I think Freud first of all really did introduce seriously the notion that there are forces which determine what we do, or drive what we do, of which we are unaware, this is a basic. Before that, writers and artists had certainly talked in this way, but Freud gave it the credibility of science through his way of dealing with it. Second, he produced a methodology by which we can get at these forces. Third, I think there really was in Freud this fundamental notion that the truth will set you free. Or the truth will cure you. Also another basic question was that Freud opened up what had been givens. You know, that men are men and women are women. Freud said in essence 'no', as you said in the quote, 'men have to be constructed.' Each man over again in each in generation and each woman is going to be constructed. And I think in addition to that the essence in each person will construct an inner structure and an inner truth of their own. It's not that the world just acts on you and then you are some kind of stamped-out pattern. There is a construction that will go on in the mind. All of those things I think are a great contribution.

Ignatieff: But what's missing?

Miller: What I think is missing is not so much 19th century but still with us. In essence Freud's theory reflected a very basic premise in our culture, and that is that men become men by having to make themselves progressively separated out from other people, in order, in the end, to become masters, or dominants. That, to me, is the story, the Freudian story. How does one become a separate person in order to become the master? And this derives basically, I think, from a social condition in which half of the human race had to become masters. And if you're going to become a master, you have to learn how to separate from the true flow of human feelings and connections.

Ignatieff: Janine Chasseguet-Smirgel, how do you react to that, way at all?

Miller: Well, first of all, women are not supposed to become that kind of a master. So women would inevitably not have this prescribed course. And, again in the broadest terms, for all societies, women have been the half of the human race that have been providing what I think is the essence of humanity: that is, connection, but that all of this has been obscured by these prescriptions about what a person should be, and the person was the model of the man. So in a short version, that's what I think.

Ignatieff: Janine Chasseguet-Smirgel, how do you react to that, that tendering of accounts with Freud?

Chasseguet-Smirgel: I would first stress what is there, not only what is missing. What is there is first of all what Jean Baker Miller said: that he was able to listen to women. But not only that. His first cases were cases of hysteria, and in spite of the fact that he stressed very strongly and against his time that hysteria could be found in men as well. His first cases were cases of women, and in a way women contributed to the creation of psychoanalysis. And the way he speaks of his cases is very respectful to women. I think that what is missing is really that he could not take into account female sexuality as being a sexuality in its own right, with its own specificities.

In my opinion it has to do, amongst other things, with the fact that his main articles on femininity had been written in '25, '31, '33 and so on, and that it coincides with his introduction of the death instinct in psychoanalysis. And often the introduction of the death instinct has been connected with his cancer. But I think that we have to think that these articles on female sexuality have also to do with his fear of death. In my opinion he did not take into account enough how the image of the mother, as being, amongst other things, the image of death, has an importance in the unconscious, and that he took for granted the reactions towards and against the almighty mother in the unconscious, especially when he was confronted with death. And he did not try to go under this image and to find the almighty mother under the despised woman, who is its opposite, so to speak.

Ignatieff: It's interesting that this period in which the *Essays on Female Sexuality* were written is a period in which his own mother dies. And that can't be unimportant. I think it's interesting to connect the death instinct and some of the essays on female sexuality. But Juliet Mitchell, come in at this point.

Mitchell: Yes, well I agree and disagree with both what Jean and Janine have said. I think in a way it's important that we should establish what we think Freud said, because we're talking around an absence at the moment. I agree that one has to go back to the early work on hysteria. And what's interesting there, as you say, Janine, is that he went along with an unpopular tendency that said 'look, there is male hysteria.' And from that he questioned the whole relationship, not only between femininity and the hysteric, but the relationship between femininity and masculinity as well, and found his friend Fliess's notion of bisexuality so absolutely fundamental.

The notion of psychological bisexuality, that we move across a line between masculinity and femininity, all of us, in different ways, would seem to me to fit in very well with the quote that you started with, De Beauvoir, that we are not born but made a woman. Freud also said, when he was attacked for his views on femininity — which I'll come to in a minute — he said 'but psychoanalysis cannot say what a woman *is*, only how she comes into being from a child with a bisexual disposition.' And so both boys and girls psychologically start off with the possibility of ending up one or other side of this line which divides masculinity and femininity. In Freud's theory, because of his observations about hysteria, we start, not with two discrete entities, male-masculine, female-feminine, but femininity and masculinity is always only a relationship between the two terms. You can't have a desert island with only women on it, it wouldn't mean anything — psychologically speaking. You couldn't have people who were just feminine, or people who were on a desert island who were just masculine. The terms are meaningless without each other.

Ignatieff: Before we go further, because that's the foundation stone of the Freudian theory of feminine — (to Miller) — do you agree with that? That it's all relational?

Miller: I think not quite in the same way, probably. See I think what we really, even in all our thinking, have been able to construct is a notion of personhood which has been overwhelmingly then described as masculine. Everything bad, everything that's seen as to be afraid of, like death, weakness, stripped of one's personhood, tends to get labelled 'feminine', in a kind of basic sense. So I think that it's very — I don't know — you can see why I'm having trouble — it's been a masculine world that's constructed notions of what is masculinity and what is femininity, and we don't know what they are. We know only what we've had so far in our constructions in our head.

Ignatieff: But would you grant that we start with that bisexual possibility?

Miller: Yes.

Ignatieff: That we don't start in some kind of *natural* way feminine or masculine?

Miller: Right. I absolutely agree. You do start with the biology. But what's then made of that biology is what is the big issue and the big question. And the biology certainly does not determine masculinity and femininity. Those are very different, much more complex levels of organisation. That I certainly agree.

Mitchell: I think, Jean, where I would disagree with that is that it is only about that construction that we can talk. After all, we can fantasise, we can have utopian possibilities of something beyond the construction, but what we have got is that construction. And I think that what is important for me about what you're saying about 'it's all been constructed along a male model,' is Freud's theory seems to me to be right in the sense that, yes, we are constructed, boys and girls are initially constructed along a male model. That the libido is male, in the sense that the small child is in the same relationship, whatever its biological sense, to the mother, and that small child up to 3-4, pre-Oedipal child or whatever, I don't need to be specific chronologically, but that very small child in its relationship to the mother fulfils something that the mother hasn't got. And what the mother hasn't got is the sex that she's, by that point not. So the mother who has become feminine because she's grown up, so to speak, what she is not is the other sex: masculine. So the little child fulfils what's missing for the mother. Because you don't fulfil something that the person's already got, there's no point, you only fulfil what's missing. And it's in the fantasies of the child that completes the mother that the masculinity or maleness of that small child, whatever the biological sex, comes into question I think.

Miller: But there your central point is what's missing, and I'm not so sure that's the central thing to focus on. That is, in Freudian theory, the central thing to focus on, but that's a whole big issue in itself, I think. Is that the critical or crucial thing, what's missing? I would say no.

Ignatieff: And your point there is that there is a tendency to define femininity in terms of absence, in terms of what's missing?

Miller: Yes.

Ignatieff: And you'd start from what's there?

Miller: What's there. Which I think is there in children of both sexes in relationship to the mother. And you know, it's the mother because the mother is the one who has had traditionally the responsibility for interacting with infants and young children, so it's the mother. But I think what they both have are tremendous capacities to relate to each other.

Ignatieff: They being both male and female.

Miller: Babies and mothers.

Ignatieff: Right.

Miller: And both contribute tremendously to that relationship. You see, I think we haven't even begun to look into that, except some people have, because we've been focused on what's missing. And very often that comes to be what's missing in the girl child.

Ignatieff: Janine, what do you make of this?

Chasseguet-Smirgel: Yes, I think that the account Juliet gave of Freud's views are re-read through new psychoanalysts such as Lacan, and I think that the main debate in the thirties was about his view that a girl and boy are both male, psychically are male. And that a girl ignores that she has a vagina and the boy ignores that the girl has a vagina, and very soon the girl discovers that she lacks a penis and then she wants to get this penis. And then she has a whole working through of this need for a penis, which is mainly a narcissistic need. It's not to complete her mother, or to be the object of her mother as a phallus, but she needs the penis as a narcissistic lack in herself.

Ignatieff: Before you go further. 'She needs the penis as a narcissistic lack in herself,' what do you mean exactly?

Chasseguet-Smirgel: Freud says it's a perception, she sees the boy has something she has not. She immediately wants it, through direct perception. And the result of this is that she wants this penis from her mother first, because she thinks everybody has a penis, that she's the only one who has not. And she soon discovers that her mother is lacking a penis, that she can't give her a penis. Then she tries to get it from her father. And she replaces finally her need for a penis by a need for a child. So her motherhood is based on a male desire. On the desire to get a penis. And this was the main controversy in the thirties because other psychoanalysts — maybe we shall return afterwards to them — thought that a girl was a girl from the beginning and that she was not a truncated, a castrated little man.

Mitchell: Janine, can I come in here? Because I think that there's — I don't disagree with what you're saying there. There's a way in which if one puts it all like that it sounds pretty crazy. It sounds like a mad theory. And that bothers me, because I don't think it is a mad theory. And I think it has some truth in it.

Ignatieff: But you don't think it's a mad theory either, do you?

Chasseguet-Smirgel: I think it's not so mad, but I think there are some deep reasons in men *and* in women — I would like to come back to this — to believe in such a theory.

Mitchell: I just want to ask one question about it, because we could go on for ever arguing about details of the theory. But in your book on perversion, for example, I think it's there, you also talk about men envying the penis. Now, this isn't very dominant in psychoanalytic literature but I think you're quite right and I want to use this to illustrate why it's not so mad that girls should envy the penis if boys can, or men can too. What is being envied is potency.

Chasseguet-Smirgel: Of course.

Mitchell: Potency is a fantasy in the mind of the child. Now, girls have to relate to that potency which the father has got in relation to the mother in a different way from which boys have to relate to the potency of the father in relation to the mother. In your cases of perverse men you get back to a boy's infantile fantasy whereby he can't grow up, that little boy, to think he'll one day be like daddy and have a potent penis with a woman of his own. That perverse little boy envies the father's penis and regresses back to an earlier position, which I won't go into now.

Now, what you'd ascribe to perverse men, is I think also ascribed in our societies to the construction of femininity normatively. Not naturally, but normatively. That the little girl's penis envy is for her femininity normative. For the boy, the same penis envy is a perversion. But it's not that one has penis envy and the other doesn't, they fit into different stages of normative development.

Ignatieff: Your clinical experience wouldn't confirm that would it?

Chasseguet-Smirgel: Yes, I can give some clinical vignettes about penis envy in women. I think they have different roots, but if you'll allow me, I shall give my opinion about penis envy in women. A young woman dreamt that she had in her hand the penis of her lover, without the lover, only the penis.

Ignatieff: Just the penis, not the lover.

Chasseguet-Smirgel: And she could suck it, she could masturbate it, she could play with it, and she was extremely satisfied with the idea that she had something wonderful in her hand and that she could not suffer any more loss, because she had the penis without the man, without the complicated relationship with the man. Another example is a parapraxis.

Ignatieff: Now, let's stop, stop, stop! Parapraxis? Help us out Juliet.

Mitchell: Slips of the tongue.

Chasseguet-Smirgel: No, a bungled action.

Ignatieff: If I was to knock over this glass there might be a significance attached to it which we could trace back to psychoanalytic motives?

Chasseguet-Smirgel: Exactly. So one of my patients, after having dealt with the idea that she had the same relationship with me as she had with her father, being afraid that I could judge her in a bad way, which she was afraid of with her father, she left my office taking my pen with her. She brought it back afterwards, but it was clear in her material that it was a way of taking something important, narcissistically-invested symbol of potency that she was taking from me but as a father.

Ignatieff: (to Miller) I can sense you want to come in and I have a sense that in this discussion what you're resisting — and I don't mean that in any psychoanalytic sense, but in purely intellectual —

Miller: Of course not.

Ignatieff: — is the sense that these are theories of femininity that are constructed around a lack, an absence, and are constructed around a masculine pole, the penis, the phallus, construed either symbolically as potency or in actuality. Is that what I'm sensing in your reactions?

Miller: Yes. In my view, the other big contribution that Freud made — I mean I haven't said them all in the beginning — was that Freud created a special arena in which one was encouraged to talk about those things which one is not allowed to talk about in the usual social level of intercourse. Again, I don't think that arena is totally free of its own restrictions and so on, but anyhow it was different. And when you begin to create such an arena, I think what you probably find — and this is what Erikson once said — is whatever society at that time is not allowing to be expressed but that really means important things to people, you begin to hear.

I think what Freud began to hear was first of all an emotional level of discourse, as it were. I mean, things not in the rules of so-called rational discourse. Emotions. He heard about this whole kalaidoscope of feelings. He heard about bodily things, which include sexual, which again you don't talk about this way usually. He heard about childish things. He heard about all sorts of weakness and fear. And he heard about people's yearning for each other. What Freud's great genius was actually was about psychological things. But he always put things in these biological terms. So you talk about penises and this and that and breasts, where he's really talking about much more complex things.

Ignatieff: But just before — I can sense both of you want to comment — you've talked negatively, let's talk positively. Some of your work refers to a notion of primary femininity, as a possible alternative way of going at this. That is, instead of talking about what women lack, talk about what women have.

Miller: Right.

Ignatieff: Now, in what sense do they *have* primary femininity? I mean, what does this term mean?

Miller: Well I don't know that that term is really mine so much. It's a term that's been raised to talk about the girl having a sexuality sort of inherently from herself, not derived from the lack of the male sexuality. Janine described it, that everybody's masculine until the Oedipal complex which makes the real big difference.

Chasseguet-Smirgel: I don't agree with this.

Miller: Yes, but that was Freud's — that's at least many people's conception of Freud's — let me say first what I myself am at least most interested in pursuing, and really exploring and studying, is really the nature of human connection and how we encompass difference. I think this is again basic to this whole discussion. And I think the thing, I mean the only source of all psychological development, is the connection between one person and another. For children, it's between adults and children. Now this has both all the possibilities for good and evil. And that in essence it's women — not totally — but it's been women's assigned place to provide this connection in truth, as it were. That is, connection with what's really happening in the kind of flow of feelings and thoughts.

Ignatieff: But you say they're assigned that role.

Miller: They have been.

Ignatieff: But if you connect it back to the notion of primary femininity, are you saying that there's some natural capacity for connectedness in women?

Miller: No.

Ignatieff: No? This is acquired and learned?

Miller: I believe. I mean, this is one of those things. I think it has been so discouraged in men, men's line of development has had such an emphasis on separating in order to be one's masterful own self, that many of these possibilities have been cut off, indeed punished in men. So that I think men are prematurely and throughout life cut off from fullest connection. So I don't at all think it goes with being biologically a woman. I mean, who knows? But it certainly has been encourged in women and called 'womanly'.

Women are concerned with relationships, everybody would say that. But I think in a deep sense it's true. Women have been in this part of life in a fuller way, granted always with distortions because women live under a family, which is under a culture, which has been under the head of the man, but even so, whatever has contributed in essence to growth — I mean, people grow only out of interaction, nobody grows in an isolated room — this whole interchange and the flow of authentic, true emotion-cum-thought, because there's no emotion without content, is the realm that women have been doing while nobody has really taken it seriously and said 'wait, look, this is the most important thing.'

Chasseguet-Smirgel: I would like to comment on this because it's related to what Jean said. In my opinion, there is a primary femininity, but it does not mean that there is no penis envy, but I'll try to explain what is the main motive for the penis envy in women. I think that the mother in the unconscious is extremely potent because of the prematurity and the helplessness of the little newborn, and that she controls him. He depends entirely on her, or on her substitute. The man's little offspring can't survive without his mother or without somebody playing her role. And at a certain moment in order to become independent of her, and in order also to acquire something which can compete with her being almighty, he wants to have something she has not. So at that moment he thinks that maybe the father can compete with the mother, and he wants to get what his father has and what his mother has not. And then he, or she, suffers from the penis envy. And I think that it's, so to speak, a secondary step which is extremely important. It's not only negative. It's a step towards independence, towards autonomy.

Ignatieff: Just on that point — the theory of a woman being the sex without the penis actively reassures both a female and a male child in the face of the immense power of the mother. Is that what you're saying?

Chasseguet-Smirgel: Exactly.

Ignatieff: That's the positive aspect of it, and that's what you're saying?

Chasseguet-Smirgel: Exactly. And it's positive and in a way negative, because I think that women have this position in society, because it does not come *ex nihilo*, in my opinion it comes mainly because of their omnipotency when they are mothers and when the child is so small. That men and women want to suppress women because of this. And what is interesting is that most of the dreadful articles written in psychoanalysis about female sexuality are written by women, not by men. These articles give a worse idea of the female fate than Freud's articles.

Ignatieff: And they do so in, in your view, because they neglect this mother?

Chasseguet-Smirgel: Because I think they have in them this need of lowering the mother's potency. And many women in the society — I don't think that they only reflect a man's position — many women don't like to obey other women, to have a woman as a boss in their business. It's not only the men, it's also a female position.

Mitchell: But I think that's actually one of the differences between the construction of femininity and the construction of masculinity, that, thinking clinically, among patients I would say that it's women who have a more terrifying imago of the mother. This is — we're talking generally — not always the case, but I mean, the witch is quite a common mother figure for a woman.

Chasseguet-Smirgel: Absolutely.

Mitchell: And this I would see as the girl having, so to speak, to stay in the relationship, to an identification with the mother, having to stay in that, in Freud's terms, pre-Oedipal phase more. Having to regress to it more, so that she retains, if you like, the more frightening dimension of the mother than the boy.

Ignatieff: (to Miller) Now, you, it seems to me, speaking for you before you speak for yourself, I think have a different, more nurturant sense of the mother. We have the witch here, we have some terrifying images of the mother. What image of the mother comes through in your clinical practice with women?

Miller: Certainly many women have big problems with their mothers, there's no question about that. But I think there are other reasons for it. Let me give you one clinical story that a colleague told me about. A little girl who was about three was walking with her father and they went into some side door of a theatre, and the man manager immediately scolded the father and said 'You can't come in here, don't you know that? Get out.' And she remembers being so shocked that this adored father — and the father was compliant — was shocked to see her adored father treated that way and responding in that way.

On the other hand, her father treated her mother that way all the time, you know. Somehow this didn't become a question in the same way. That's so regular, has been in so many families. And I think that bespeaks we are all so used to having women treated that way in one way or another that little girls then would much rather stay stuck with seeing the problem around their mother than — these days, I think that perhaps it was different in more patriarchal families in the past — than to really question the whole role of the father and the father-mother relationship in the family setting. So I find with women patients, they can go on and on forever about their bad mothers and blaming their mothers, and you have to find ways to get past that.

Ignatieff: To the father-mother relation?

Miller: Right. Which is much harder.

Ignatieff: Let's leave that issue here because there's another issue that's been floating through this discussion. I hear you saying, Jean, very clearly throughout we'd have different men and women, different notions of sexuality in a different society. That is, I hear a very strong sense that the gender roles are socially constructed in an unequal, patriarchal society. There are things we can do to change that, but we have to keep our gaze firmly fixed on the social. I also hear that self-evidently in both of your discussions, but I hear a very different inflection, and I think it's Juliet's position that I find most difficult to figure out. You are a socialist, a feminist and an analyst. I wonder what sense you have of what can be socially changed. You're in the clinical situation dealing with people at the very kind of deepest inner roots of the self. How does the social impinge as a clinical experience and what can we do about the social? Because I think that's where I'd like us to take the discussion.

Mitchell: Well, nobody is not social. So everything that we're talking about comes through the filter of everybody's particular social experience, and that will be different if you're a victim of a holocaust or an upper class member of the aristocracy in England, or if you're black or white or male or female. I mean, everything that we're talking about comes through the particular experience, which is a social experience.

Now, in terms of changing within a clinical setting, I suppose — this vexed question of what is a cure etc — greater tolerance for parts of oneself, greater acceptance of something that one's whole life has been so restricted because it's been so unconsciously forbidden to one. Some greater play with ideas. Ability to play, perhaps, a bit more. Play with thinking, play with relationships. That sort of possibility, both in personal relationships and in work situations. I suppose if anybody achieves more freedom within that context I would think that we'd done some good work. And I would say socially that is true too.

But I would make a distinction here between what I think is the importance of playing with ideas, socially, playing with political ideas, and being able to use utopian notions. Now, I think that utopian notions are based on some infantile experience. They must be, you know, we can't think from nothing. I mean, we have to have something good in our experience to think from too. And I think that some of what Jean is saying is the utopian dimension from which we can all think and fantasise and which is terribly important politically. I don't give it a sort of place on the outer edge.

Ignatieff: But what do you mean utopian, more practically in the domain of sexual relations and gender relations?

Mitchell: Well I think Jean's envisaging a society where there is much more free play between sexual identities. Where we're not so fixed, in terms not only of masculinity and femininity, but in terms of dominance-subservience, with the masculine as the dominant and the feminine as the subservient. And we are not in a society in which we have excluded as secondary all the qualities that are regarded as feminine, which includes all the best qualities of kindness, caring, nurturance, relationships, protectiveness, communication, all sorts of things. Those mustn't become subservient qualities, they must become, if not equal, then dominant. I mean, they should be the important ones. And the qualities of hardness and separation and domination which are associated with masculinity must shrink. But you get into a sort of tautology there because it is exactly dominance that is being asked to become subservient.

Miller: No, but relinquished

Mitchell: Well that's even more of a tautology. I mean, then what is dominant? You're asking for a society that is truly egalitarian without any structures of dominance. And I don't think we have seen yet a society which is truly egalitarian without any structures of dominance. Now, whether we then start envisaging a society which has different structures of dominance, and then we have different structures of subservience too, seems to me just to invert the problem.

Ignatieff: We've started two hares running at once. One, the question of social transformation, but also the more narrow one of what it is possible to achieve within the analytic session. And those are two allied questions in a sense, but I'm just wondering, Janine, how you take these questions. Freud said the best we can hope for is to convert hysterical misery into common unhappiness in the clinical session. We've had a very interesting view of clinical practice producing a kind of inner tolerance, an inner playfulness, which then has political consequences —

Mitchell: Of self and others you see.

Ignatieff: Yes. Which then produces a transformed self in relation to others. I mean, what would your agenda be for transformation?

Chasseguet-Smirgel: I am a bit pessimistic, I must say. I think that on the individual level, psychoanalysis can do a lot. And one thing you have not added to your list of what psychoanalysis can do is to create the possibility of freedom of thought. But it's an ideal. The second thing is about my pessimism. Which is — it's not entirely pessimistic — but, for example, I happened to think about the fact that women, before, let me say, 20 years ago or 30 years ago, were so afraid of having a baby without being married. They even committed suicide because of this. It was a terrible shame. And I wondered what had changed. Is it really that our behaviour as women or as men has really changed towards women? I think it's not our behaviour which has changed but the fact that contraception is possible, is free. That means that a woman who has a baby without being married has chosen this. She has chosen to have this baby. And I think it changes absolutely our relationship to this fact.

But what I want to stress is that our deep view of passivity, I am afraid it has not changed. You understand what I mean? I mean that a woman who has now a child without being married, she's active, she's supposed to have been active. It is supposed to have been her choice. She has not been given up abandoned like a thing. She really has chosen this. So what I mean is that it's not our feelings which have really changed, but her situation has changed because she is supposed to have chosen this. So I don't know if it's pessimistic or optimistic, because in a way it has changed.

Mitchell: In a Freudian sense you would say that she was now being active and masculine in what she is doing.

Chasseguet-Smirgel: I would not totally confuse activity with femininity, but I would say that she's active, she's considered by the others as being active in her choice. And that has changed. So I don't know if it's a pessimistic or an optimistic view.

Mitchell: Well, we are getting back to the position whereby Freud's notion of the repudiation of femininity because femininity is associated with passivity, that's historically, by connotation, by vocabulary and first — the word first comes into the language in the 17th century in England as 'he was of so uncertain and passive and feminine a disposition.' It's in Clarendon's history and it's a he. And that's where feminine comes in as a word into English, as meaning passive. So it's the connotation and the association which is also a position. It's a position in relation to parents, to fathers, of being passive, which is associated with the feminine that we are still repudiating. So if we accept women in different, more tolerant ways, different ways from 100 years ago, it's because they have taken over more masculine, i.e. active, positions. That's really what you're saying. There is social change, but somewhere there isn't psychological change commensurate with the social change, I think is what you're saying.

Ignatieff: (to Miller) Is that your sense as well? We've had massive — not adequate — but we have had great institutional change for women without concomitant inner psychological change at the same pace. Is that a judgement you'd share?

Miller: By and large. I think it's a mixed picture. I mean, I think we have had, first of all not so massive, I mean nowhere near as much as I would like, but on the other hand some things have changed very much, even in 10-15 years, at least in the United States. But these psychological constructions are not so easily changed. I think most of us have — certainly I grew up long before I ever knew of such a thing as anything could be different between men and women. And then we raised our children and they received, you know, the psychological representations of our minds and incorporated them in their minds. So the deep-seated things are harder to change. Much harder. But I want to give a sense of a mixed picture. That there has been change which to me in my lifetime would have been inconceivable. It's been so great. In the sense often that women have of themselves and the value of other women. On the other hand it's nowhere near what I would see as a total, you know, flourishing of the psychological possibilities of women at all. And I don't think that can change without a concomitant change in the structures in which we live.

Ignatieff: Two final quick comments, because we're coming to the end. Janine, do you have anything to add to what you've said?

Chasseguet-Smirgel: Well, I would like to stress the fact that psychoanalysts in general agree on a lot of different points within psychoanalysis, and it's very striking that about this question of female sexuality they still are not in agreement after about one century of practice. And I think personally that it has to do with our relationship towards our mother. And I think that in men as well as in women one of the main conflicts is with their mother and that, for instance, passivity is first experienced with the mother. And after the women are supposed to be passive, I think that's because she was so active with us. At least we have the impression that she was so active with us when we were helpless.

Ignatieff: A final comment Juliet.

Mitchell: Well, I suppose I'm pessimistic in the sense that I think that all societies have to construct some way of symbolising sexual difference, the difference between the sexes. And we don't know of societies in which that difference doesn't also have a degree of deference in the relationship. That difference has historically not been on a level — meaningful difference — of course you can have a difference between two glasses, one of which is blue and one of which is red, but that's not meaningful difference. Meaningful difference has implied some sort of hierarchy hitherto. And that's my worry, that's my pessimism. I can't envisage a society in which sexual difference will not be in some way symbolised. I think Jean does envisage it in a way. But in so far as that's what's at stake, then I think we've got a very long way to go and I can't really see the future.

Ignatieff: That's I think where we should leave it. I think you've heard an absolutely fascinating debate, perhaps the most fascinating area of modern psychoanalytic thought. And I think it shows something: psychoanalysis is not a technique, not a toolbox. Freud opened up the site for a cultural debate about the deepest roots of our identity, our gender identity. I think one of the things you've seen tonight is the sense in which Freud made it possible, often with very bad, often even with incorrect terms, made it possible for women to speak for themselves, to articulate their own differences, and in effect to force men to begin to think about their own difference as well.

CHAPTER 5

Psychoanalysis: Nothing Sacred?

Michael Ignatieff with Philip Rieff
Sherry Turkle and Geoffrey Hartman

Ignatieff: Good evening. What we need to get to grips with tonight is just how radical Freud's influence on our culture has been. For some, this impact has been profoundly liberating. He's freed us from old inhibitions, especially in his frankness about sexuality. And his moral style, his respect for irony and complexity, his honesty and tolerance, has helped us to be reconciled to the darkest sides of ourselves. But for others, the freedom Freud has brought us is double-edged. In his frankness they see the slippery slope into permissiveness: in his iconoclasm, the heresy that nothing in human life is sacred. For these critics, Freud has encouraged a dangerous illusion that we can choose our own identities and indulge our desires as we see fit. Followed to its logical conclusion, Freudian freedom has contributed to the fragility of modern marriage, and to the weakening of respect for legitimate authority.

So the question: what has Freud done to us? To our sense of ourselves and to our attitudes towards authority? To discuss these questions I have with me Philip Rieff, Professor of Sociology at the University of Pennsylvania and author of two extremely important books: *The Mind of the Moralist* and *The Triumph of the Therapeutic*; and Geoffrey Hartman, Professor of Comparative Literature at Yale and a deconstructionist who has taken up Freud as one of the subversive modern masters; and Sherry Turkle, author of *Psychoanalytic Politics* and more recently *The Second Self*, where she asks whether Freud's models of the mind are being edged out by new discoveries, especially in Artificial Intelligence and computers?

Well, let's begin with this question of the sacred. All of you in different ways are talking about the sense in which after Freud nothing is sacred. Now we need to know what that means. And to begin with you, Philip Rieff, what do you think it means?

Rieff: I would say that we had until modernity a culture of command. Or of commandment. This was treated by many a writer, many a poet, many a philosopher, and Freud saw in his patients that the culture of command from an absolute authority above, the commander, or in Kafka's language in the Penal Colony or the Punishment Colony, the commandant, was really at the end of its effectiveness. His patients were suffering, he thought, from failed prohibitions. The instrument of those prohibitions, which came from revelation, was repression. And there is an interesting symmetry, to conclude this preliminary survey of what Western culture, and indeed all cultures are. These elements at the very top of the vertical of authority were too much for many of his patients to carry. They were suffering from failures of obedience. Failures that he tried to correct. So I would say where theology was, in everyone, least of all the theologians, but nevertheless in everyone, there therapy had to be. He was responding to a culture of command at the end of its capacity to command in the highest. That is the prohibitional commands, 'do nots'.

Ignatieff: The ambivalence I hear there is whether you're saying that Freud is responsible for the desacralisation of the authority of command or whether he, as it were, appears at a moment when that authority of command is already in big trouble. I'm just wondering whether Geoffrey Hartman or Sherry Turkle can come in on that issue?

Hartman: I would agree with Philip that Freud establishes our most current, to my mind most acceptable, critique of moral responsibility, or rather of authority. It's a critique, because, as you suggest, he is not saying that there can be absolute freedom, he is not saying that prohibitions are not necessary, but he feels that we've entered an era where this kind of authoritative prohibition is failing and imposing psychologically a tremendous burden. He is not exactly someone who wishes to remove burdens, but to go through the path of knowledge, as if knowledge itself could make — the burden that knowledge imposes is a different kind of burden than the sheer weight of prohibition imposes. If I may add one more thing very fast: for me, the nothing sacred, in a very popular or in a very routine matter, is that certain feelings, certain emotions that we may not hold as sacred but we certainly put in a certain area of appreciation and innocence, he casts a shadow on. I remember Lou Andreas-Salome in her journal where she records —

Ignatieff: She's one of the early Freudians. Someone who corresponds with Nietzsche and with Freud.

Hartman: That is right. And at the very late age of 50 she met Freud and he changed her life. She is sitting with him listening to Otto Rank, also a follower and disciple in fact, and with whom he had a very filial relation, less competitive than with Adler and some of the others. He was talking about regicide and Freud passes her a note saying the reason why Rank is so devoted, or can remain so devoted to me is that he can rid himself of the negative side of his feelings towards me by talking about regicide. This is just as an instance of how a certain shadow, interesting shadow, is cast over love, other emotions of that kind.

Ignatieff: Yes. Sherry Turkle, do you want to come in on this issue of the sacred, what has been left desacralised by Freud?

Turkle: I think that Freud is subversive and psychoanalysis delivers a subversive message in so far as it calls into question what each of us, as individual actors, have as our commonsense understanding of what it's like to spend a day in the world. That is to say, that we are centred actors, we make our decisions, we're out there as kind of autonomous acting egos. That things are as they seem, and that we can know reality. And most people, even in the 20th century, post-Freud, have these sort of three reassuring rules of realism as their way of getting around their day. And Freud says, 'You can't do that. Wait a minute, that's not true. Those three things are not true. You're not an autonomous actor, things are not as they seem, and you really can never fully know the reality.' And it seems to me it's in that subversion of the most commonsense ego psychology to which we all cling that he is a subversive figure. And other philosophies, other philosophers, have delivered this message. And the difference it seems to me about psychoanalysis is that it's a philosophy in everyday life. You have to confront it when you confront the slip, when you confront your dream, when you confront these very tangible pieces of the everyday that Freud casts into shadow and exhorts you to use as windows onto this other reality.

Rieff: But his analytic edge came in the period that seems for certain classes, the cultivated classes, over. The absolute prohibition, the 'shalt nots', are not so powerful perhaps now as they were were when Freud began what he thought of, I think, as a mission.

Ignatieff: But on this question of the 'shalt nots', I hear a very different inflection here. I hear you saying, Philip Rieff, that in a sense the loss of the shalt nots, the de-legitimation of the 'shalt nots' in which Freud takes part, is a matter ultimately to be regretted. I hear the two of you saying something very different, which is that pressure had to be taken off. It's put us in a very much darker relation to ourselves. We now are not so clear what we shalt not do. We're also not so clear about what we shall do. But your take on this move is much more positive, it seems to me. The de-sacralisation of those prohibitions is emphatically a positive thing, in contrast to what I hear Philip Rieff saying. Or am I caricaturing here?

Rieff: It only means that Geoffrey and Sherry are both subversives.

Hartman: It means that I respond to Philip as Philip responds to Freud, in terms of a mythology. That I feel within Philip Rieff a certain modified pathos for a position which is no longer accessible to me.

Ignatieff: By pathos you mean a nostalgia?

Hartman: The way he used it, yes.

Rieff: The history of Freud's old testament is a history of terrible disobediences and excusing reasons. History in that respect hasn't changed all that much. What has changed is the sense of willingness to obey an authority that Freud literally dissolved in the transference authority. It wasn't that he himself was anti-authoritarian in some romantic way. Some authority had stuck in some way that had proved costly to the life of the patient. The world patient was known to the prophets and was known to Augustine, there are passages in the sermons about the world patient stretched out on the table of the world. The illness that the Augustines and that the prophets saw were the illnesses of transgression. The illness that Freud saw was the illness of too powerful a conscience, too submissive a will to commands that no longer held. Not that we moderns, Freud's patients, were the first to be stretched out by these disobediences.

Ignatieff: But what I can't understand is why you can't rejoice in the fact that Freud encounters people who are being made ill by the force of their conscience and attempts, as you say, in the transference relation in analysis, to loosen that pressure. Why do you regret that attempt to loosen the weight of Victorian repression?

Rieff: Well to call it Victorian repression is —

Ignatieff: Well that raises another issue, but repression.

Rieff: He was after a god that was much older than the Victorian god, indeed. The authority that had been received by this culture, a definite authority of what it was we were and were not to do, had become an enormous problem and these late members of Western culture, what I would call modernity, were suffering from moral demands much too imposing, much too strenuous for them. They simply were not, or indeed in a very complicated way, no longer obedient in a history of humanity that had begun, he thought, in his mythologising version of our culture, with a crime, with a transgression. But the sacred remains there. What has happened is that we are to live far more analytically in the middle range.

Ignatieff: What do you mean, middle range?

Rieff: What I would call — in the vertical of authority, beneath the prohibitions there were always circumstances, excusing reasons, hypocrisies, particular modes of excusing oneself from the inherited obediences that had emerged as symptoms rather than as faith. And these bad faiths, these imperfect pieties, which had always occurred, were sick-making, and the thing to do is to examine the duality in us that made us pay a price for particular disobediences by examining the life history of the vengeance wrought for a particular disobedience.

Turkle: Perhaps there's a question of what you lay at Freud's door and what you don't. It seems to me that there's another way to look at the story, which is to say, not that the Freudian vision led to these abdications of authority, but rather that at a moment in the history of the culture, or in the history of a culture, a society when these — and this is certainly suggested by your own work — when the glue of large social prohibitions, of large social institutions, the Church, the State, capital S, begins to get unglued, unstuck, when the centre doesn't hold in that sense, psychoanalysis is there to help people create a personal mythology, a sense of personal meaning when these larger social ideologies can no longer provide that sense of coherent meaning in biography.

Ignatieff: Geoffrey Hartman come in here.

Hartman: Yes, I think Sherry raises an important point. I would perhaps rephrase it this way: that psychoanalysis certainly helps in that sense the individual towards a new type of coherence, whether or not you can analogise that to a personal mythology. But the question which is raised by Philip Rieff vis-a-vis that, is whether you can have a culture in the strongest sense of psychoanalysis. I mean, what kind of institutions on a social level can psychoanalysis institute? And I think Philip once said in *The Mind of the Moralist* that it is no longer the church and state which are the institutions but the hospital.

Rieff: The hospital theatre.

Hartman: All right. I think you add that now, the hospital theatre. And that's part of the problem. I think what you say is right. But when we think of culture — not in the sense of what we do in our daily lives, which I think by the way is a very important Freudianism, has something to do with the psychopathology, or if you wish, with the philosophy of daily life — but if you think of it in terms of Philip Rieff, as a larger social institution, say, it is a problem.

Ignatieff: And the problem is that you have a culture which creates a very individualistic kind of knowledge, namely psychoanalysis which is —

Hartman: That's not the problem in my view but that you can't transit from that to a larger holding pattern. Because the hospital doesn't seem to us, or the hospital theatre, doesn't seem to us a good basis for a larger model to which we owe our allegiance or in which we want to live and breathe and have our being.

Rieff: Exactly. But think of two cases. One I saw recently, a public case in Washington, a meeting of the American Psychiatric Association. There was yet another proposal to put into the manual used by all psychiatrists — in which psychoanalytic theory is very important, whatever the particular acceptances and rejections — there was yet another move which was, if I may put it this way, aborted swiftly before the first phase went too far, to call rape a paraphilic coercive disorder. Making it a sickness, when that act of violence was in the Western tradition understood, you remember Paul's phrase, the body is the temple of god. Whatever the Jews and the Christians did to themselves and each other, it remained the absolute command that a violation of the body was a transgression. That was the true sickness, transgression. To call that transgression, rape, to propose seriously at the American Psychiatric Association that it be called a paraphilic coercive disorder, is itself a symptom of something that defeats Freud. Freud had no such intention of course. But this powerful attack on the interdicts in itself —

Ignatieff: An attack which takes the form of essentially converting a moral transgression into a medical pathology, an illicit conversion of a transgression into a medical pathology.

Rieff: More than a moral transgression, a transgression against existence. Against the way things are in a commanded culture. And another example, a case from among Freud's cases. A teenager, whom he called Dora, you recall. Fascinating struggle, a brilliant struggle between this superb man, this genius, fairly early on in his career, and this teenage girl whose father's mistress' husband was after her. And she refused to join this erotic game, had all sorts of pains, hysterical symptoms. And in time Freud says in a moment that might be called a supra-Freudian slip, 'I've seen Herr K, he's rather prepossessing.'

Ignatieff: Why's he saying that?

Rieff: Freud is saying that in a passing moment when his own guard slips. He lives within the fastness of his own world, it is quite unclear that these accusations about his relations to his sister-in-law and all of that cycle of debunking —

Ignatieff: But the point there is that Dora is resisting for very good reasons and Freud is saying to her, this man is prepossessing. What's your problem?

Rieff: No, he's saying more than that. He's saying you're really in love with your father's mistress who is the wife of the man who is after you. And you won't admit your teenage lesbian love for this woman, at which point she flees.

Hartman: Dora is one of the most problematic cases, one of the most moving cases of the early Freud, but surely one of the most problematic cases, in which you feel his suggestiveness, Freud's suggestiveness. What one critic recently has called his epistemological promiscuity. That he is, as it were, suggesting to her certain things that do not come out all that clearly from her mind.

And one is most uneasy, at least I am very uneasy in reading that case history.

Ignatieff: But let's focus on what's making you uneasy. Because as I understand the pairing of these two examples, that is, the rape example and the Dora example, what you're objecting to in the consequences of the Freudian tradition is the ways in which a set of moral acts are illicitly converted into a set of medical pathologies, and in a sense excused as such.

Rieff: Excused, and yet Freud wasn't proposing that she solve her aches and pains, which were very serious, by joining the incestuous circle. He simply wants her to be aware, simply; it's a Herculean task. He wants her to know what the issues really are. She is unaware of the issues. But then imagine a culture that begins to have a very popular sense of the issues in which, without licence from the old boy himself — who looks a bit like Geoffrey — without licence from the old boy, there are incest therapy movements. The Swedish parliament has a committee lowering the age at which incest is statutorially to be brought to the attention of the authorities. The long Scandinavian nights. There are all sorts of problems. Geoffrey used the word problematic. The trouble then becomes, as my secretary once, a dear lady in California, said to me when I was writing a piece which was rather severe on Adolf Hitler, she came in and said in a post-Freudian moment of farce, with tears streaming down her generous cheeks, 'Oh professor Rieff, you're so severe on Hitler. He must have had a terrible childhood.'

Turkle: That makes the point.

Rieff: That makes the point.

Turkle: I think that it's possible to have a Freudian scepticism and a psychoanalytic eye on the reality behind the reality.

Rieff: Absolutely.

Turkle: Without causing that to condone rape, incest, acts that a culture can continue to experience as illegal, immoral, not the way in which human beings want to live with each other.

Ignatieff: That is it is possible to understand psychoanalytically without pardoning everything morally?

Turkle: Yes.

Rieff: Wonderfully possible.

Turkle: It's possible, but I think that in the story you tell there's the suggestion of the, what did you call it, the slippery slide from one to the other that I don't think is a kind of necessary condition of living in a post-Freudian world.

Ignatieff: Why do you think it's not a necessary condition? Because these are strong cases. What makes you so hopeful?

Hartman: I don't think we've worked this out. And I think Sherry is saying this is what we are in the process of working out.

Turkle: Well I agree, I think we're working it out. But I think that what Freud contributes is to work it out with a clearer view of what's really involved in our humanity. I believe in a psychoanalytic compassion as well as a psychoanalytic scepticism. Or a psychoanalytic liberation. I mean, there's a sense of a different kind of compassion.

Ignatieff: What does psychoanalytic compassion mean? What do you mean?

Turkle: That we all suffer from the same processes, some of us merely suffer more than others. And that these processes are the fundamental tensions and ambivalences that are set up by our earliest lives as children growing up in a family. That we have mothers, that we have fathers, that we are in triangles, that that's hard, that we're ambivalent, that we love, that we hate, and that we are sexual, that it's not so clear if we're in control at all times when we want to be. I mean, I think that the fact that we are little while others are big, will have a profound impact on the way in which we see justice and morality for the rest of our days.

Rieff: Always been the case Sherry. The parent question, which is where Freud tries to stop as clinician, as a genius of the clinic, of the very hospital theatre that is modernity, he stops at the parent question. As in certain readings one can say he stopped Hamlet and the question of parents.

Ignatieff: What do you mean by the parent question? Just for clarity?

Rieff: The question of the sexual wishes of the child as it relates to the mother.

Hartman: The Oedipus complex.

Rieff: And to the Oedipus complex. But Oedipus, the King, had a father who was one of mythology's, or history's great transgressives. He was one of the first great homosexuals. And Laius the king is himself a transgressive, an immoralist. And his son blames the gods of course, carries Antigone with him. Hamlet, whom Freud treats as a great second case of the parent question of humanity, our relation to our parents, has concealed behind it what I'd like to call rather not the question of parents, which is *the* great Freudian question of parental authority, but the parent question of humanity, which is the sacred. That is, is there anything beyond the parent? Is there any authority standing beyond the super-ego?

Ego is the agent of reality. If you have a reality of our sort, a reality in fragments, a reality that can take you in any number of directions, if you free us for choice, then the question remains of the right choice. And I think that the right choice is precisely — and the parents, the question of parents — is precisely where Freud, short of his mythological consolations which don't really work for me any more than they do for you or did for Freud, I think, the question of parents conceals behind it, in a pre-Freudian and post-Freudian way, the parent question of humanity, which can be put in this sentence: am I thy master or art thou mine?

Turkle: Perhaps I think it takes psychoanalysis, or Freud's contribution, too narrowly in terms of its impact on all of us today, to focus on this parent question, the issue of interdiction, the issue of authority, at the expense, for example, of saying, what did Althusser say, that the crux of that new science was the discovery of this new object of study, his epistemological break, the discovery of the unconscious as an object of a new science, of a new study. Focusing on the discovery of the unconscious, I think you come out with a very different view of what the impact on the culture is than if you focus only on the discovery of a too-rigid set of prohibitions that people needed to struggle with.

Ignatieff: Just before I let Geoffrey come in, I think you should explore that thought further. If you focus on the unconscious as Freud's chief contribution, and not on his impact on authority, you get a different reading of his impact. Now what's different?

Turkle: Well I think that we've talked about Freud as revolutionary. The debate as to whether Freud is revolutionary or not revolutionary has tended to be waged in terms of sexuality. Was he revolutionary on sex or not? It seems to me that the question of free will is for us today what sex was to the Victorians. That same urgency about issues of sexuality and interdictions about sexuality that so tormented the Victorian spirit, we are now tormented by questions having to do with whether or not we are actors, our own centre, whether, to take the computer examples, whether we are programmed from the outside. In what sense are we like or not like machines? In sociobiology it raises the question in what sense are we like or not like animals, in a very serious way. It seems to me that fields of study like Artificial Intelligence, like sociobiology, the use of computer metaphors to describe people in everyday parlance, much as psychoanalysis was picked up in everyday parlance — 'I'm debugging a relationship' — that kind of talk, raises the issue of free will and to the extent to which we are actors in a very urgent, hot way. And that Freud remains an urgent and a hot thinker, not just for the contribution about sexuality, the family, the question of parents, but by this discovery of the unconscious which makes us take seriously a way of talking about this sense in which we are not our own centre.

Rieff: I don't think that that is what is happening. I think that the self, the ego, the agent of reality, is being de-centred, fragmented. The ego derived from Exodus 3:14, in which the ego of egos said to his first analyst 'I am that I am.' That 'I' has been derived from that

'I' in the history of this culture, and it is that 'I' that is yielding to an incredibly complex reality in which you become, as Nietzsche called it, your role faith at the moment. 'You can be anything, man, just anything. You can do anything.' A Johns Hopkins Medical Professor said in an interview 'I think we can beat this thing called death.'

Ignatieff: Geoffrey Hartman, I have a very strong sense when I listen to this beautifully expressed Jeremiad about the decentred self that you, on the contrary, have a modernist's welcome for the decentred self, but perhaps we should in fact define the decentred self more carefully first of all.

Hartman: Everything I'm going to say will sound like a cliche on this matter.

Turkle: Geoffrey also likes the centred self.

Hartman: Exactly, I do, I'm totally incoherent. I may be coherent maybe personally, but incoherent philosophically. The way I understand Freudian culture, if we can use that term, that is not philosophy, but the way it meets us, or we meet it, almost day by day, the kind of thing that Sherry was referring to at the beginning, is that we have a greater — that's why I say it's a cliche — greater tolerance for ambiguity and ambivalence. We look at ambivalence and where we don't see ambivalence we go through a method of supposing ambivalence. And this method I think is very important. It's a spiritual exercise. That doesn't mean that we should or can stay ambivalent, but I think this is part of how Freud has, if you wish, programmed us. He says you must pass through this spiritual method and suppose that human actions are over-determined, in other words, perhaps ambivalent. I know they're not exactly the same. And in that sense you can talk about the decentred self.

Ignatieff: Could you just define over-determination as you're using it there?

Hartman: Yes, that you cannot delude yourself, or you should not delude yourself for too long that all your motives are traceable to a single origin and usually a high-minded or pure origin.

Turkle: I love this image of a kind of new discipline, a new strategy, that you subject yourself and other people to, focusing not on just the limitations of self-knowledge, but on the need to pursue it even asymptomatically to that point that you can, to go as far as you can in giving yourself a hard time. I think this is an extremely important part of what it means to live in a psychoanalytic culture.

In addition, I think there's a commitment to the idea that behind the message there is a meaning. For example, consider the difference — this perhaps comes from teaching at MIT — but consider the difference when I get up to lecture in front of my class and I make a slip, I make a Freudian slip which I am analysing in terms — and am embarrassed, because to me it reveals the window onto my soul, it's a royal road to my unconscious — but consider the difference between my appreciation of the Freudian slip and my students', who say to me it's just an information processing error. It's just a programme being derailed when I make an error. And it seems to me that the essence of living in the psychoanalytic culture is the meaning, is to focus on the meaning. You subject yourself to this discipline that gives you a hard time, that focuses on ambivalence and that demands at least a search for the meaning behind the message.

Rieff: And where does the meaning stop? That is, is the meaning of the repressive unconscious, which is the unconscious we're all talking about, the second unconscious? There is the instinctual unconscious, there is the repressive unconscious out of which these occasional slips of yours occur.

Turkle: Repressive or repressed? Did you make a slip?

Rieff: No, I don't think so. Because I think that there's, as Freud himself noted at one point, there's a third unconscious. And that third unconscious he said he daren't plumb. That was early on, you may recall. And it's that third unconscious, if I may put it in a literary reference that Freud himself would have liked, is Hamlet's problem. Hamlet is aware in his conversation with Laertes before the final duel and the death of all in contact, that it was not 'I', Hamlet, 'twas Hamlet's enemies or Hamlet's enemy. There are any number of Hamlet's enemies who are Hamlet. But when he says, I think, 'to be or not to be,' he is asking do I belong? To what being, to what sacred order do I belong? And I think he has a question about belonging, as does Freud.

Turkle: But Freud would say you belong to your own history. You're inexorably bound.

Rieff: Well that's a hopeless condition.

Ignatieff: Why hopeless?

Rieff: Well I think it is hopeless because it is a kind of brilliant egomania to say you belong to yourself. That self, he himself thought had an immemorial history that hadn't died for which he had to invent the primal crime, he had to invent the non-Jewish Moses, he had to do all sorts of things to begin his history.

Turkle: But you see Philip, I think he didn't do so well when he went into those inventions to try to bolster that intolerable situation. I think that really facing the implications of his thought and the implications of what it is to live in the modern world, is to not have to start to invent all that and to accept that in fact we are left with only our history. And whether or not Freud had trouble with the implications of his own vision, I think that where psychoanalysis has — and this in the constructive sense from my point of view — left us, is with not a complacency, but a resignation to the fact that we each only have our own history. And that that may be very painful, and that makes it very hard, and there is a certain amount of nostalgia that many people feel about when it might have been otherwise, but that's the story.

Rieff: I reject that nostalgia entirely. It's not a question of nostalgia, it's a question of whether you belong to something larger, greater and more commanding than your own Hamlet.

Turkle: I think Freud would say that the well-analysed person, this myth of the well-analysed person, this fiction of the well-analysed person, is someone who can face what you're describing as this impossible situation, to face being a father when there's no father on top and to say 'I'm gonna muddle through'.

Hartman: Or to be a split personality of a certain kind, ambivalent situation.

Turkle: I'm gonna do the best I can. I see the Freudian message as a message of struggle, of giving yourself a hard time, and of struggle.

Rieff: It's a great virtuoso performance. The Nuremburg rallies, that whole theatre, that entire erotically massive hospital theatre of Nazi Germany was modernity at the end of its tether. And it is that condition of Murder Incorporated that I think describes the virtuoso world at which point Freud died in 1939, with his death work *Moses and Monotheism*.

Turkle: And I would say that Freud's vision of the well-analysed person would have so understood the massively eroticised relationship with his or her own father that the appeal of this nightmare father would have been less. But there's a salvation to this, there is an image of a salvation for modern man and women in the myth of this well-analysed person. This is a person who can handle this.

Rieff: What's the salvation?

Turkle: It's a person who can handle this new living without a god.

Hartman: There are no panaceas. We agree there is no absolute therapy. The only place I think where we disagree is the role of institutions and of our relation to institutions. It seems that's a critical difference here.

Ignatieff: I think you're narrowing the difference there, (to Rieff) and I don't think you'd agree with that.

Rieff: I don't agree. Because I think you can identify up in the manner that the world out of which Freud himself came tried to do. Quite in bloody ways, but nevertheless making the same identification in the transference relation is to transform the therapist into the father. You can identify up. You can also identify down. It's an empty mechanism. This massive identification down is itself a function of modernity, and we in the West have been identifying down steadily once the identification up was de-legitimated.

Turkle: But analysis is not just transference. Up or down, analysis is more than identification. Analysis is understanding.

Rieff: Is the resolution of the transference, is it not?

Turkle: Analysis is understanding what's going on, so that you can have some control over your life in a situation of great complexity, great paradox.

Rieff: And you can have an analytic community culture?

Turkel: I think we have one. In other words, I think that when I said salvation or when I start to substitute salvation for muddling through, what I mean to say is there is this idea in psychoanalysis of not the good mother but the good enough mother. In other words, a mother that will give you enough to let you function; of a culture that will give you enough to let you function. I think that what we're living today are people doing the best they can with this new material which is modernity, and I think it starts to look a lot like what Geoffrey was starting to sketch out, that is to say you know you're decentred and certainly Geoffrey writes about that very eloquently. On the other hand you also sense a moral self, a communal self and you do the best you can to put those together, under duress. But I think Freud tries to present tools for doing that with compassion towards oneself and towards other people.

Hartman: I don't think Sherry or I would be saying that we are making a para-religion, even though you use salvation and that's symptomatic — I know, I didn't say it — but she caught her slip, you see she caught her slip and says when I say salvation I realise and so on. You're not substituting, not substituting Freud as the father, god of a new religion, you understand that. But that he's so essential — we're trying to get at why he is so essential an ingredient of contemporary thought. What we're fighting about in a sense is the very image of Freud. What we're fighting about here is Freud himself as, I can't quite say a role model because Sherry will say then that it raises the question of direct identification. Nevertheless to some extent we are fighting about the role image but perhaps not quite within the concept of sacred order, since we feel that — at least I feel — that the term 'sacred' has a historical valence, but I feel shy about speaking of the sacred and I think that within Freud the emphasis is mainly not on the necessity but on the fact of profanation. Not that it's behind but it's on the fact of profanation.

Rieff: I would say that the churches are empty in their god-talk and in their ethical talk, that they are themselves paratherapeutic institutions. I am making no case for the contemporary religiosi. As

I see them, they're fellow travellers of the therapeutic. That does not mean, however, that those who were true to the struggle, the eternal human struggle, not to identification but to truth, understanding fully that Freud's truths have their own language but are by no means sprung from nowhere, they have themselves a para-sacred character, they're negational truths and this negational truth-telling will not do, I suggest, for cultures, for communities. Whether this experiment of modernity will itself succeed in allowing us to muddle through a death that is very near is a question that we all know is very near. We know of no culture before that has engaged so ruthlessly in the experiment of having nothing sacred, of belonging to nothing, of having negative communities.

Turkle: I think it would be a disservice to Freud and the psychoanalytic vision to present it as a vision ultimately of a kind of solipsism. A negative community may be a good enough community for a self that is well armed for the struggle.

Ignatieff: A final word Philip Rieff.

Rieff: That virtuoso performer, the analytically sophisticated and wise self cannot constitute a culture. I think that it's demonstrably an impossible culture. And an aestheticising analytical culture that will allow endless transgression. That is the problem. I haven't been attacking Freud. Freud responded to the real condition he saw. That real condition has worsened, not gotten better, and the Freudian response will not serve the culture — which was I thought our subject not Freud, as such Freud is a hero of mine. He's a negational genius — stopping short of — because he was no prophet and the age of prophecy has ended, just as Weber was no prophet — but to call this night the best we can do and to speak of modern parents as we now see them as somehow in their 'tolerance,' a word Geoffrey used, in the ambiguities, that is not good enough, I think. It really isn't. You said good enough. It's not good enough.

Ignatieff: I think we're going to leave it there at this moment with everybody champing to continue the discussion.

Hartman: It's not good enough.

Ignatieff: It's not good enough but it will have to do. We've had a very, very stark and I think crucially important disagreement here. It's clear from what we said that Freud's most dramatic effect on this culture is in our sense of ourselves, in an understanding of the vocabulary of our motives, and some of us here are saying that that knowledge is the best we can do. It teaches us to give ourselves, as Sherry Turkle said earlier, a hard time and it teaches us a stoic knowledge in a world in which nothing is sacred. We've also heard a much starker view of the modern self left to us by Freud and it's this virtuoso performer, the clown on the high wire, alone, without persuasive reasons, but going on nonetheless. That's the disagreement we have had tonight and I hope you've enjoyed the discussion.

CHAPTER 6

Psychoanalysis After Freud

Michael Ignatieff with Steven Marcus
Hanna Segal and Arnon Bentovim

Ignatieff: Good evening. The founder of psychoanalysis has been dead for almost 50 years. In this last programe of our current series we want to look at what's happened to psychoanalysis since Freud. Some argue that the last 50 years have been a period of breakthrough and innovation. New methods of treating children and new kinds of patients, new theories of the mother-infant relationship and major new figures like Melanie Klein, Anna Freud and Donald Winnicott. But others argue just as strongly that the world of psychoanalysis has become like Miss Havisham's home, a world stuck in the past, sterile, turned in upon itself. According to these critics, the exciting developments have been outside psychoanalysis, in the emergence of new drug treatments for mental disorder, and in the growth of rival schools of therapy which emphasise people's real problems in the here and now, rather than the inner world of a patient's fantasy. So the question: is there still life in the Freudian Empire? Is it still at the cutting edge of therapeutic insight?

To discuss these issues I have with me Professor Steven Marcus, an American literary critic whose book, *Freud and the Culture of Psychoanalysis*, is often sharply critical of the state of American analysis; Hanna Segal, a leading Kleinian analyst who has written some of the most important accounts of the work of Melanie Klein; and Arnon Bentovim, consultant psychiatrist at Great Ormond Street Children's Hospital and a leading family therapist, well known for his work on incest.

Professor Marcus, I thought we should begin with you and this question of the cultural vitality of psychoanalysis. In your book you seem to be arguing strongly that psychoanalysis is on the decline as an institution and is on the wane as a cultural force. Am I right?

Marcus: Well, I think you're generally right, if you look at it in a comparative sense. If we go back to the years following World War Two, at least in the United States, psychoanalysis as an institution enjoyed at that point, and for at least 20 or 25 years after, unequalled status, prestige and prosperity, both as a therapy, as a sub-discipline clinically of medicine, and as an instrument of critical understanding and research. It had very high cultural status, both for people who are patients and for people who are interested in the theory and the clinical problems that were attached to it, and for the kind of light that it threw on certain cultural problems as well. There's been no question, it seems to me, that in the last 15 years that prestige has begun to wane, to be challenged, both from within and from without, and that both organisationally, especially, and in some sense intellectually, psychoanalysis, at least in the United States, is in, I wouldn't say a state of complete disarray, but is not nearly so self-confident nor so neatly put together as it was 30 or 35 years ago.

Ignatieff: Just before I bring in Hanna Segal and Arnon Bentovim, can you elaborate on this, on its cultural place? You've talked about the decline of it as an institution, but psychoanalysis is a source of metaphors of self-understanding of the culture as a whole, and what's the state of play there in the United States?

Marcus: Well, it seems to me that psychoanalysis is the most elaborately developed and complex form of introspection that we have developed in Western culture. And it's a direct outcome of the tradition of introspection in Western culture, starting with the Greeks and coming up to now. And it's a secular form of introspection, and it has as its aim the understanding or the mostly rational understanding of those things or forces within us and without that are not rational. Its step ahead was to take as its subject those things which are irrational in us, which do not make sense to us or which we tend to deny or overlook and subject them to some sort of rational analysis and explanation.

Now it seems to me that the power of this is connected with the power of its origins. That is to say it has its origins in 19th century middle class culture, which had a very powerful belief in rationality, in introspection, in the effectiveness of the self as an agent of change, let's say, and that if one looks at the current state of affairs in advanced societies of today, one finds that a number of these cultural forces have been attenuated, if not lost, weakened if not entirely disappeared. And that some of these values which we connect with middle class society and culture and its various kinds of institutional offshoots are no longer in the same central position of strength and authority as they were before. Such as, let's say, Freud's simple notion — and it was a very pragmatic one — that functionally he would define health, let's say, as the ability to work and to love. These virtues, which we do connect, it seems to me, with the culture of the past, do not themselves have an unproblematical status, in our culture.

Ignatieff: I'm going to want to come back to this sense that the crisis of psychoanalysis is tied up with a crisis in high bourgeois culture and its key values. But before we get onto that I want to ask

Hanna Segal how she reacts to this rather critical diagnosis of the state of a discipline which she's been such a distinguished member of for most of her life.

Segal: Yes, it always is difficult to have challenged that way something one has invested one's life in. I think first of all that there are differences between developments in the United States and here. One is that in the United States it's a purely medical organisation, and, as you say, they consider themselves as psychiatrists who happen to have another qualification. It is something completely different here. Our membership is about one third lay. But even those of us who are doctors do not consider ourselves, except some, as sort of doctors who happen to have this instrument, we consider ourselves psychoanalysts.

The second thing has to do with success. I think that one thing that killed psychoanalysis in America is its success, and particularly the social and financial success. For instance, it's characteristic that in England psychoanalysts are not a very well paid profession. So if you go for a career, if you go for money, if you go for success, then psychoanalysis nowadays is not for you — and let's be thankful for that.

Now, the exciting developments here had to do with Klein and Winnicott and people like that and with the analysis of small children, revealing an extraordinary wealth of early experience, and also revealing that certain things, which in Freud's time were thought to get structured at the age of seven or eight, get structured very much earlier on.

Ignatieff: What do you mean there?

Segal: I mean there, for instance, that Freud speaks of the introjection of the father and the superego happening around latency.

Ignatieff: Latency being 11 and 12 years old

Segal: No, being sort of seven to pre-puberty. Now, when Klein started analysing little children, she found that there was quite a complicated internal world already, having to do with the earlier relationship to mother, with feeding, with the triangular situation. It's usually thought that Klein leaves out the father. In fact she brings the father in much earlier, because she brings in the triangular relation to the parents, and the state of the parental relationship — whether father is a supporting agent to mother or not, very much earlier on. And that opens the way to certain, I would say, depths of the psyche, to the importance of fantasy — by which I don't mean that the external things are not important, but that it's not a matter of the trauma falling on a child that is a *tabula rasa*. Nor is it the case of a child fantasising and the environment doesn't matter, but one saw this interplay between what is internal

— the child's desires, fantasies, fear which coloured his perception. And I think nowadays cognitive psychologists and neuropsychologists are with us in saying there's no such thing as a perception. It's always perception through scanning, through projection of expectation. So when we are told that our work was out of keeping with psychologists and neurophysiologists they're catching up on us, like they're catching up on us that the infant has a meaningful relationship, I think, from day one.

Ignatieff: (To Bentovim) You must be chafing at the bit at this point to add your own sense of the map of what's happened to Freud, and what are the developments in your particular area that seem to matter most.

Bentovim: Well, I was very interested in what Steven was saying about the American context, because I think I would agree with Hanna that the English context is a very different one, and I suppose I would be probably seen as one of the doctors, in our particular context here, who've, in a sense, used psychoanalysis as instrument, rather than become identified with psychoanalyst as identity. I think it's true to say that there's always been much more of a struggle within psychiatric institutions in terms of the role of psychoanalysis — in my training in the Maudsley in the early Sixties, the struggle to get a dynamic voice heard, against a very powerful orthodox group of psychiatric thinkers.

Ignatieff: What do you mean by dynamic voice?

Bentovim: Well the notion, I think, as Steven was saying, that the apparently irrational isn't because of a psychotic process, but it is rational when looked at taking a different set of ideas about what the phenomena is saying, what the person is saying. That there's method in madness, that the psychotic thinking, that the neurotic behaviour has a great deal of meaning if one understands it from the history of the individual and his experiences.

And I also think that certainly I would identify very much with the fact that I grew up in a context where psychoanalysts were talking about application to groups, applications to institutions, and where it was very easy for me, from the influence of people like Winnicott and Kleinian ideas, to make the shift, if you like, to say well what my interest is is not just the way in which I, as the psychoanalyst, I as the therapist, have put on to me the context of the child, his relationships which are played out with me in the work with the child, but to take another step to say well perhaps we should look at the context as a whole, not just the way that the individual reflects his experiences, but the way that that individual is having his experiences reinforced constantly within the context. Which of course coincided with another paradigm which I think also became very popular in the United States, which I think is not an offshoot of psychoanalytic thinking, but would be seen as a different paradigm — the notion of a systems paradigm which looks at the organisations not in terms of the psychotic processes which Hanna was talking about, but in terms of the way in which groups of people organise themselves. So that in a sense the individual is not just reflecting his own biography, his own experiences, but in fact is also showing disorder and disturbance because of the way in which he's being treated here and now, within the system within which he's living.

Ingnatieff: Hanna Segal, is this a legitimate extension of psychoanalytic tradition, this emphasis on systematic therapy and systematic interventions, or do you regard this as a kind of heresy? Don't mince words

Segal: No, no, I'm not there to sort of legislate what's proper and orthodox, what isn't. It's mostly what's creative and where do new insights come from. The way I like to think of it, there's a lovely song of Chesterton's which says 'I don't mind where the water goes if it doesn't go into my wine.' What I mean by that is it's all right to put wine in the water, but please don't bring water into the vats where the wine is made because nobody will have any wine either for themselves or in their water. I think psychoanalysis is absolutely unique as a method of research, of acquiring knowledge, and if we dilute that by getting mixed up with all sorts of method, then those vats in which, as it were, the stuff is produced will just stop functioning. On the other hand wine should go into the water. I think we should go into the world with our analytical armoury and apply it, because obviously not everybody can have psychoanalysis, apply it in any way we can, but we should see to it that our own depth of understanding, our own capacity to bear the transference and so on are not interfered with.

Ignatieff: But on this precise point it seems to me that the metaphor, the water in the wine, to get back to this earlier thing, is making a very strong claim that in fact psychoanalysis is the orthodoxy against which systems theories and other late additions should be judged and I'm surprised that you're so tolerant under this very heavy claim. Because it seems to me it's up to you to justify to me, for example, as a layman, why it is that an individual-based therapy is so much deeper than a systems-based, because a layman in the street thinks 'well if the problem's in the family we'd better deal with the family.' So tell me why exactly.

Segal: I think actually, if I stick my neck out — I always do — I think that for most mental disorders the treatment of choice is actually psychoanalytic. Let's say, if a child is disturbed and was in a disturbed family, on your old model I would like the parents treated; if it's very bad I would like them separated. But it seems to me that however much we are in a group, that from the time of

Freud's structural theory we know that there is an internal structure in the individual and that the individual will not change unless something in this internal structure changes.

Bentovim: But I would say that I would not see this as a treatment of choice, because I feel that we need instruments to be able to, if you like, analyse in a different sense, not in the psychoanalytic way.

Segal: The family as a structure.

Bentovim: Well, not just the family as a structure but the context which relates to the individual, because I suppose I would take a view that in fact if you change the context you can often change the individual. I think where, for me, the role, if you like, of the more individual-based treatments is where basically I've in a sense been able to change the context and quite clearly the individual hasn't changed.

Marcus: In so far as one is interested in the nature of subjective experience, that is subjective individual experience, the two areas where one has to go to learn most about it are one, literature and two, if you want to understand the systematic study of subjective experience, psychoanalysis is, as we say in America, the only game in town, really. Because it is the most developed theory of subjective experience that we have.

Now this, it seems to me, is based again on another anterior notion, which I think Doctor Segal has been pressing towards but which I perhaps can put from another point of view, which is the belief that was very clearly accepted as an assumption in Freud and is still an assumption in psychoanalysis, the belief in the individual as the primary unit of experience. This doesn't mean that the outside world is not real, this does not mean that the family is not real, but what it does mean is that there is a primacy given to the experience of the individual self and its subjectivity. And this is, it seems to me, what psychoanalysis is based upon, what it moves toward. It does not leave out the outside world, it never leaves outside the family, it does not leave outside history or context or anything like that, but what it insists upon is not only the primary existence of the self but the primary agency of the self. That the self is an active agent and a responsible agent in its own dealings with both itself and the outside world.

Ignatieff: But how do you react to the claim of systems therapists who insist that that presumption is wrong?

Marcus: Well, I think that I react with disagreement theoretically. Pragmatically it seems to me that it depends on what they're doing and what the situation is, and if in fact a systems approach will work therapeutically why should I be opposed to it? But it seems to me that theoretically there is another case to be made and that psychoanalysis is it seems to me 'deeper' with achieve this kind of mastery, let's say, in a relative degree of course, of one's feeling. Now it seems to me that in so far as contextuality and interaction goes, there is now, at any rate, an enormous amount of that in the activities of psychoanalysis. That is to say the fundamental activity, or one of the fundamental activities in a psychoanalytic situation, is the analysis of transference and counter-transference. And that is contextual and relational all the time. Now you're saying, I think, that you want to broaden the context and so on. But what I have not seen yet is anything that looks like a comprehensive theory, as it were, of this kind of activity which can challenge what psychoanalytic theory is, in so far as depth and comprehensiveness and range are concerned

Bentovim: It's interesting that you see the present gurus in the systems thinkers, are actually going to other biologists, people like certainly Gregory Bateson, previously Materana, who really in a way talks about domains and different domains in which the observer is playing an integral part, in which the definition of the situation actually creates realities. And I think that this is where certainly systems thinkers are interested, is the subjective creation of reality, and I think they would probably argue that the notion of being the captain of one's soul may be another illusion.

Segal: Yes, of course, very exaggerated. But I was thinking of that as opposite to this idea that individuals don't exist, they're a function of the group.

Marcus: That they're purely relational.

Segal: Or that they are a passive function of the group. And then one wonders whether the individuals in the group are also passive. But obviously one is never captain of one's soul, that is an illusion. But to the degree in which it is possible, feeling responsible for one's own part. Which is the essential part of being responsible for oneself. Even in concentration camps we know that individuals went through it differently.

Bentovim: You see, one of the things, if I can think very specifically, one of the issues that we find, working in the field of sexual abuse, incest, is the issue of responsibility. You see, a father will say 'well, she seduced me.' And there's a real problem for instance, because of, maybe misunderstandings, but certainly popular notions about that, the sexual life of children, that children are not abused, that the — you know, the way in which the early notions of Freud's seduction theory are being looked at and saying he rejected seduction theory and said it was the child's sexual wishes, I mean, which has had such a very distorting effect. But that of course fits into the family, where the father says 'well, you know, all right, I know that I touched her first and maybe I shouldn't have, but then she came to me, so she has a responsibility.'

quotation marks around it and anterior in its insistence upon the self and the existence of the self. Now we know that today in advanced cultural studies and philosophy the very existence of the self as an agent is being doubted. I mean, if we look to the Continent and so on the self is an agent that is as it were an evanescent phenomenon. I don't believe in that, I don't think that is necessarily true, and it seems to me that one of the strengths of psychoanalysis is precisely its insistence upon the primacy of the self as an existent responsible active agent here.

Bentovim: I think I would agree with you that there's no question that in terms of exploration of subjective experience that's right. But the problem is, it is a theory which arises out of a context isn't it? It's a theory which arises out of a context of me and you, of a two-person relationship where the definition is one is a listener and a responder and where the other is an active participant. And I suppose that if you change the field, say, as Gregory Bateson did, to observing the interaction, then in a sense you have a different domain of experience which arises because that would argue that mind in fact only arises in interaction, rather than as an internal experience. And I just wonder whether one of the problems is that the theory has arisen — I mean I would agree with you there's a difference between it as a theory and a theory of practice — but that it is a theory which arises out of a particular context. And if you take another step and look at the context, which is the interaction of the psychoanalyst and patient, maybe you then could develop a different theory which is of interaction rather than of individual.

Segal: Well the whole point is that it's not a different view, that the whose basis of the psychoanalytical since Freud discovered transference we know that everything is an interaction. The point is you can study it in greater detail in the psychoanalytical thing. But I want also to reply to what you said about this view of a person that is a passive recipient of group forces, and I think that one of the things that goes, from my point of view, wrong in the culture is that we invest more and more in the group and therefore we become passive recipients. And I agree with you that Freud insists the individual is crucial from a certain special point of view. I think a psychoanalytical treatment aims at making a person be captain of his soul, and not have this passive relation.

Marcus: I just wanted to make two remarks. One is your quotation comes from a poem by Henley, who is a late Victorian poet.

Ignatieff: The Captain of the Soul.

Marcus: The Captain of the Soul. 'I am the master of my fate, I am the captain of my soul.' It's contemporary with Freud. Contemporary with Freud's notion of the self too, that one can

Segal: She wanted it.

Bentovim: She wanted it. She has a responsibility. And I think the issue of sorting out within the context of the family and the social context, where responsibility lies, that in fact parents have to be responsible, children can be active, but that in fact adults have to be responsible and so on.

Segal: That goes without saying. But it seems to me that there is another point. I don't go along with Masson that Freud discarded this theory for wrong reasons. Because, after all, thousands of analysts after confirmed Freud's idea of infantile sexuality. Because whilst we discovered that there's more incest, more child abuse than Freud would admit, I don't believe that all neurosis and psychosis comes from that because if child abuse was as common as neurosis, psychosis and so on, it would be the norm.

Bentovim: Well, there's some would say that it's very common.

Ignatieff: I think we need some mapping here, because we're moving very rapidly in very difficult terrain. First of all we've talked about the contrast between individual based therapies and therapies that are —

Segal: Not therapies, psychoanalysis.

Ignatieff: Psychoanalysis.

Segal: I don't like the word 'therapy'.

Ignatieff: And group-based, systems-based interventions.

Bentovim: Context-based.

Ignatieff: And there's a fundamental disagreement about where you should intervene. Now, the second issue which is being introduced now maps onto that. Which is to say, do you intervene with the reality of a patient, primarily, or do you concentrate on the way in which that reality is symbolised in the interior? The intra-psychic dimensions of that reality. And it seems to me there's a fundamental disagreement in post-Freudian psychoanalytic thinking about this issue: where to place the emphasis between reality and fantasy in one's interventions and in one's theory.

Segal: To me it's a little bit of a wrong question. It's like the chicken and the egg. There is a view attributed to Klein that she attributed everything to fantasy. There is a view, I don't know if it's right, attributed to Winnicott, that everything is trauma from the outside. It seems to me, I cannot answer this question, I am concerned with the interaction in all sorts of ways. But I think what is therapeutic actually — I'm not speaking of children mind you, you might have to change the environment, which is quite a different thing. I mean, many very psychoanalytic child psychiatrists will say first of all the child must go to the boarding school or first the parents have to be treated, the child will adjust — but once there is a deep disturbance, which is already structuralised, becomes part of the self, that only dealing with the structure will fundamentally alter —

Ignatieff: The psychic structure.

Segal: Not remove the symptom, but let's say change the psychic structure in, one hopes, a lasting way. But in dealing with the structure, I always deal both with what is external, in the sense of what I have done to which the patient reacts, — including mistakes — and internal, what he attributes to me which can be shown to come from the past. And gradually in the past, when you do that in the transference, the past almost without intervention clarifies 'I thought I was guilty for my mother's doing' and so on 'but I can see very clearly now that she was a depressed woman when I was a child and that's how I reacted.' So to me the question is it external or is it internal, you know, it's like saying do we breathe oxygen or do we breathe a mixture?

Ignatieff: But surely the question is of very real import in therapy?

Bentovim: Well I think, you see, that it's interesting that when you were replying, Hanna, you in a way brought in a specific context, which is that you were saying 'yes, there are certain situations where it's quite clear.' The difficulty is to define when is the deep disturbance needing a sort of intervention diagnostically or in fact — you see, the way that I would approach, say, a child, even presenting with a deep disturbance, would in a sense be to say it may well be that what looks like the subjective experience of a deep disturbance, which almost needs the child to have a re-experiencing, because I think what you're saying is that the notion of psychoanalytic work is a re-experiencing, restructuring, the individual's experience and his views through the relation with the analyst. And I suppose that what I would say is that in fact sometimes if you take a view that a group of people who grow up together share meanings, share views — they become, if you like, a closed system which between themselves, in fact, may very well have some very distorted views where one individual has to carry for the others — that in fact although you could sort of take off the people that need that experience and give it to them, the issue is in fact, if you draw a boundary around where is the disturbance contained, that one can actually work with that total group and that in fact one can get a major shift.

I think where the difference between people whose paradigm of work is basically a psychoanalytic one would be — and I've had many arguments at the Tavistock Clinic where I also work — between individuals who say this child, this individual has a deep disturbance, but where I might say with the same context, 'I don't think so, I think that that is still a manifestation of what's going on, and in fact a change in the here and now might in fact make a very major difference which would make the sort of enormous commitment to work actually unnecessary.' Which is really what psychoanalysis with an individual implies, a tremendous investment of personal time, energy, for that individual and for that particular professional. And I think the issue of where we draw the line is a real problem.

Segal: Yes and again, do we want to be psychiatrists or do we want to be psychoanalysts? I mean that area is not an area of my major interest.

Bentovim: That's right.

Marcus: If I may say so, I think that there has been a shift also in psychoanalysis, in the sense that even classical psychoanalyses today are no longer simply reconstructions of a past history, they are extremely conscious of the here and now. That is, not only through the transference, but through one's own situation in life and so on, and one is continually going back between the here and now and the past and to see how the past is coming up in the here and now and is understood in the here and now. And so the accusation that has been levelled in the past against psychoanalysis, that it was only dealing with the past and not with the here and now, seems to me anachronistic. That's not the way things operate, even in psychoanalysis nowadays.

Now, in connection with the earlier question that you also raised, it seems to me that when Freud abandoned the seduction theory he did not say that children were not seduced. He just said this was not a universal experience, that's all. Children of course were seduced and those children who were seduced suffered traumas. But what he said was that there are also children or young people who had stories about being seduced which turned out to be fantasies and that they produced symptoms which were very much like the symptoms that were produced by people who had actually been seduced. And this beginning to sort out the relation between what could happen to you as the result of an actual experience and something very similar that could happen to you as a result of a mental experience alone, was one of the great steps in the building of psychoanalysis. Now it seems to me that there is no contradiction between that and, let's say, a therapy with more than one person.

Ignatieff: And another thing to add, presumably, is that if children are actually traumatised by sexual abuse, the Freudian theory as I understand it is that that will only have traumatic effects depending on how it is fantasised, reproduced and dealt with in the psychic interior.

Marcus: How it is processed internally.

Bentovim: I think probably the notion that a fantasy could have a traumatic effect on the individual's life, is probably one which, say, John Bowlby, who took a very pragmatic view and has in a sense produced a series of formulations about development/attachment theory which have been very heuristically helpful as far as biological and other scientists looking at interaction, looking at the development of infants have been very helpful. And in a way, his emphasis, wasn't it, was to say that the baby who clings, who seems to be behaving as though he's terrified that the mother will leave him, is in fact an infant responding to a rejecting mother. I mean, he said it very baldly. As if to say that the notion that a fantasy could have a traumatic effect, that the self could destroy its development, was in fact a misnomer. And I think that one of the problems has been that that formulation, which as you said takes a long time to work through and which other people can see in different ways, has probably had quite a major effect I think, or for a period of time, in making people neglect what people said as being real because they're just products of their own experience.

Segal: It seems to me you keep it on a very conscious level. It's not a matter of a patient saying she was seduced and a hysterical woman then — and that's what I mean, you're looking at things on that maybe a bit superficial level. I agree with Marcus that Freud's discovery that the child may have had a fantasy, and even then it was just a conscious fantasy, opened up really psychoanalysis which is our understanding of the instinctual life of the child's fantasy. And it's true that in Freud later it's clear in the Schreiber case he concentrated on the internal to the neglect of the others — it isn't true now. My feeling is that the risk is it goes the other way. And of course traumata, not just sexual abuse, much more often by neglect, cruelty, misunderstanding, but I have a feeling that that's where, let's say, I would disagree with Winnicott, certainly when confronted, you know, with everything is bad mothering, bad fathering, every detail.

But children do react differently, and how they react, of course, there is a wide range. There are mothers or fathers who are so awful that no infant could survive and develop. Then maybe somewhere there are ideal parents who are so marvellous that no infant could be neurotic. I haven't seen them. In the wide area it's a constant interplay between internal and external. And I think if you over-emphasise, over-emphasise the external, you again miss the inner reality. I've got an incest victim as a patient, I have two, but in one of them it's tremendously clear it was a stepfather when she was quite young and mother was pregnant, and all her own fantasy about mother's pregnancy and the alliance with this very weak, inadequate man — and though clearly the adult is responsible if you look at it from the outside, in her experience the traumatism was allying herself against the mother. And later a great bitterness of course with the stepfather. But unless you dealt with this inner reality, that at that moment she would do anything to destroy the pregnant mother and therefore was an easy victim, if you don't go into that and leave it at 'oh poor little thing's been seduced by the stepfather', you get nowhere.

Bentovim: I would agree. I mean, in our work unless we deal with all aspects of the relationships and the patterns — and indeed the whole focus is always on the mother as well as the father and daughter. But what I'm interested to know, or I think would be worth exploring, is the notions which emphasise, if you like, the internal experiences, do these fit in, and have they fitted into which, for instance, where people would like to say 'well we can ignore what children say? We can ignore them because basically they're living in a sort of fantasy.'

Marcus: I've never heard anybody say that. Because again you take it on such a superficial level.

Bentovim: Yes, I'm aware of that.

Segal: That if the children say they were seduced they will believe them. Certainly anybody would take them very, very seriously.

Ignatieff: I think the issue, as I listen to this, is that you haven't told us how you theorise the traumatic impact of actual events. That is, the advantage of the Freudian theory is that it is traumatic to the degree that it is given meaning within the psyche.

Marcus: And the advantage of the Freudian theory, if I may be rude and interrupt, is that there's an internal structure which is specified.

Bentovim: The way that I conceptualise, if you like, on the basis of traumatic experiences, must be that the individual has to give some sort of an explanation of why this has happened to him.

Ignatieff: To themselves.

Bentovim: To themselves. And that what actually happens is that either they in fact become identified with the sexual experience and the children become highly sexualised, or their whole internal life is blotted out and they become very frozen and they become traumatised, like a traumatised frozen child. I mean, it can go either way. And it can have a pervasive effect on their development, their development can be blocked, they can fail at school, they can have many psychosomatic complaints.

But the interesting issue, of course, is that if this is a trauma that happens within a family context, one then actually has to say 'what is the effect on the family's life?' Because on the one hand you have an individual, who for whatever reason out of his or her history, finds himself using a child sexually, treats the child sexually instead of, if you like, relating to another adult. And then as a result of the traumatic response that then feeds back on the way that the family goes on and the way that child will then maybe become further scapegoated because of his pattern of response to what actually happened to him. And this will have its own effect and may even help the way that the parents are going, so that they actually have a difficult, bad child, who is then seen as an excuse for the offence.

Segal: That's a very psychoanalytic view. That doesn't come from systems theory.

Bentovim: Yes, that's why I say that basically my understanding of what happened has to be a developmental response. The issue then comes in how do we intervene? The difficulty is that if you then take one fragment, in other words, if you work with the child who shows the deep disturbance, naturally enough you have a family context which is actually trying to ensure a major amount of secrecy, denial, not speaking about matters, putting it on the child, rejecting any attempt to work, even rejecting the work with the individual. What I'm trying to say is that the focus of one's intervention then has to be different. I think there has to be a belief that there may be qualitative differences between an actual experience that a child has and the way it develops.

Segal: That it's not so that the father is seen the same as an actual happening. But of course we shifted to child abuse because that is your field. Of course there are other traumata. I have worked with people who were children escaping from Germany and the Nazis. I mean, this is not the only game in town.

Marcus: Absolutely. And there are children who are neglected.

Segal: And children who are neglected. But see, I'm not saying that other psychotherapists are not useful. Only what I'm saying is that without psychoanalytical insight derived in detailed work in psychoanalytical interaction, you couldn't speak about the reaction to the incest in the way you were speaking.

Bentovim: Yes, I don't think I would ever deny that. The difficulty comes, what do we do then?

Ignatieff: Ladies and gentlemen, because we're drawing to a close, I want to — since Steven Marcus had the privilege of beginning — I want to return to something you said right at the beginning which puts all of this discussion in a much broader frame. You said right at the beginning that psychoanalysis' crisis of development was tied up with the crisis of high bourgeois culture, and you said specifically when Freud said we should work and love as the basis of health, that was an appeal to high bourgeois cultural values which are themselves in crisis, and that psychoanalysis can't escape that crisis. And I think as we look to the future we have to think about what you mean there and whether that's true and then ask two distinguished clinicians whether they recognise that sense of a culture in crisis in their own practical work. But could you amplify what you said at the beginning?

Marcus: I'll try. It seems to me that the cultural roots of psychoanalysis are in the liberal bourgeois culture of the late 19th century. And that its essential categories, its categories both in part of identification and description, and certainly its categories of value, of valuation, come out of that culture as well. That is to say, certain values connected, as I said, with work, with love, with the family, with rationality, with responsibility, with honesty as morality. I mean, the morality of psychoanalysis is the morality of truth-telling really. With moral uprightness of one kind or another. The kinds of things that one saw in late 19th century poetry, too, as doctrine, were in many ways connected with psychoanalysis. And these values and these categories, it seems to me, come from high liberal bourgeois culture.

Now, it's very difficult to ask a discipline whose categories are derived historically to, as it were, jack itself up by its own bootstraps and leap out of its own categories and invent new ones. So it seems to me that in so far as late 19th and early 20th century middle class culture is undergoing change, and crisis, because all change, you know, entails a crisis, and the values, let's say, of a stable family seem to be in doubt. And of all sorts of other things. For example, it's utterly unclear to me, you know, what is of better value — if you're going to make a valuation — what is better, the situation that we had in the past of miserable monogamous families, let's say, people tied together, in which the children suffered, or what we have today, which is serial monogamy or single parent families too. Both clearly produce misery, now, of one kind or another. But they produce, as it were, different kinds of misery. And I am unable to say which is better than the other, although I do know that the children in both situations suffer terribly.

However, the values that inform serial monogamy or inform a single parent society are different from the values which kept miserable monogamous families together. Now, psychoanalysis was built and grew out of those latter values, although it's had an effect in many ways in producing the second set of values too. I mean, it's not an innocent bystander, it's a participant in the changes which have partly undermined it too. Now it seems to me that 19th century middle class culture or bourgeois culture is, if we take the idea of the family and if we put next to it the idea of what's happening in education, the idea of the decline of religion as a group, and the growth of peer groups and formative influences in ways that they were not before, just limit it to those things, we do have a culture in rapid transition it seems to me, and at certain levels clearly, as far as the family goes, I think, in crisis, crisis of a different kind, let's say, than the crises that we saw in late middle class culture and that Freud was the first to diagnose. And therefore it seems to me that psychoanalysis is undergoing itself changes that are in many ways registrations and refractions of these changes in the larger culture.

Ignatieff: I need a quick comment from each of you. As distinguished clinicians do you feel this force of change beating at the doors of your — ?

Segal: Well, not being alive in Freud's time I don't know. But I would say about the sort of criteria, you know, to work and to love, which at some level is not a bad one, whatever community you live in. If you mean real love and real work. I think the culture I grew up in, the sort of Kleinian analysis, the criterion would be any shift from a paranoid-schizoid, narcissistic way of functioning to what she called the depressive way of functioning, which is the ability to relate to people as people and not as objects, and the ability to experience responsibility and guilt for what one does, that this is the basic shift one looks for.

Ignatieff: That's a kind of version of the values informing your therapeutic practice. Do you have a story to put beside that, as a final word?

Bentovim: Yes, I find it's very difficult to cap that or to know quite how to respond to the very large picture you've painted of major change. I think from my point of view, I would say that the ways in which I see social systems working together, the way in which people in intimate relationships work together, peer relationships, that the paradigms of psychoanalytic thinking, although they have a role, the issues of how one actually creates change in those systems in a way preoccupy me. How can I, if you like, make the sort of social transitions which are so common today, whether it's of divorce separation, of change of life crisis, change in a here and now way I think is what preoccupy me. In other words, it's not the question of how do we deal with our history of experiences but how can we actually find ways of making social systems function in a compassionate, caring way?

Ignatieff: I think that's where we're going to leave it. It's clear that the future of psychoanalysis depends on the dialogue that it maintains within itself, within its own divergent tendencies, and the dialogue that it maintains with movements of therapy beyond its borders. And it's clear from this discussion that the future of psychoanalytic traditions bequeathed from Freud depends on the vigour, the intensity, the passion, the honesty of those debates. And that's where we'll leave it.

Bibliography

Bettelheim, Bruno. *A Home for the Heart*, Thames & Hudson, 1974.
Freud and Man's Soul, Chatto, 1982.

Bowlby, John. *Attachment and Loss*, 3 vols. 1963-80.

Cardinal, Marie. *The Words to Say it*, Picador, 1984.

Chasseguet-Smirgel, Janine (ed.) *Female Sexuality*, Pelican, 1976.
Creativity and Perversion, Free Association Books, 1985.

Delueuze, Gilles and Guattari, Felix. *Anti-Oedipus*, 1977.

Eysenck, Hans. *Decline and Fall of the Freudian Empire*, Viking, 1985.

Freud, Sigmund. *The Standard Edition*, (24 Vols, 1953-74)
The Pelican Freud Library, (14 Vols).

Gellner, Ernest. *The Psychoanalytic Movement*, Paladin, 1985.

Green, André. *On Private Madness*, Hogarth Press, 1986.

Grosskurth, Phyllis. *Melanie Klein*, Hodder & Stoughton, 1986.

Grünbaum, Adolf. *The Foundations of Psychoanalysis: A Philosophical Critique*, University of California Press, 1984.

Hartman, Geoffrey. *Easy Pieces*, 1985.

Jones, Ernest. *The Life and Work of Sigmund Freud*, Pelican, 1984.

Kernberg, Otto. *Internal World and External Reality*, Jason Aronson, 1980.

Kohon, Gregorio (ed.) *The British School of Psychoanalysis*, Free Association Books, 1986.

Lacan, *Ecrits*, Tavistock, 1977.

Malcom, Janet. *Psychoanalysis: The Impossible Profession*, Pan, 1984.
The Freud Archives, Cape, 1984.

Marcus, Steven. *Freud and the Culture of Psychoanalysis*, Allen & Unwin, 1982.

Miller, Alice. *Thou Shalt not be Aware*, Pluto, 1985.

Miller, Jean Baker (ed.) *Psychoanalysis and Women*, 1973.
Towards a New Psychology of Women, Pelican, 1976.

Miller, Jonathan (ed.) *Freud: The Man, His World, His Influence*, Weidenfeld and Nicholson, 1961.

Mitchell, Juliet. *Women: The Longest Revolution*, Virago, 1984.
(ed.) *The Selected Writings of Melanie Klein*, Penguin/Peregrine, 1986
Psychoanalysis and Feminism, Penguin, 1986.

Ricoeur, Paul. *Freud and Philosophy*, Yale University Press, 1970.

Rieff, Philip. *Freud, The Mind of the Moralist*, 1959.
The Triumph of the Therapeutic, Penguin, 1973

Roazen, Paul. *Freud and his Followers*, Penguin/Peregrine, 1979.

Rycroft, Charles. *Psychoanalysis and Beyond*, Chatto/Tigerstripe, 1985.

Segal, Hannah. *Introduction to the Work of Melanie Klein*, (2nd ed.) 1973.
Klein, Fontana, 1979.
The Work of Hanna Segal, Jason Aronson, 1981.

Turkle, Sherry. *Psychoanalytic Politics*, NY: Basic Books, 1978.

Wollheim, Richard. *Freud*, Fontana, 1971
(co-ed) *Philosophical Essays on Freud*, CUP, 1982.